LIVING IN THE LIGHT OF HEAVEN

And bless you!

Jax Sinla

Also by Max Sinclair

Halfway to Heaven
Heaven on Your Doorstep

Living in the Light of Heaven

Max Sinclair

Hodder & Stoughton

LONDON SYDNEY AUCKLAND

British Library Cataloguing in Publication Data
A record for this book is available from the British Library

ISBN 0 340 66924 1

Typeset by Palimpsest Book Production Limited,
Polmont, Stirlingshire

Printed and bound in Great Britain by
Cox & Wyman Ltd, Reading, Berkshire

Hodder and Stoughton Ltd
A division of Hodder Headline PLC
338 Euston Road
London NW1 3BH

To Mum,
who first put a vision of heaven in my heart

and

To Sue,
whose determined daily living in the light of heaven
is a constant inspiration

Contents

Acknowledgments

Thank you . . .

Carolyn Armitage, for the initial planning and encouragement.

Sue Baldwin, my Personal Assistant extraordinaire, for typing, phoning, researching and coffee.

Anne Coomes for downsizing my original draft material mountain so that it would fit into a book.

Stuart Jones for stimulating discussions and keeping my theology on the rails.

Martin Levitt for excellent material in the section, 'Why Do We Think Like We Do?' and for not minding all my questions.

Elspeth Taylor, my editor, for skilfully shaping ideas into reality, for going the second and third mile in the editing, and for constant encouragement.

Sheila Watson, for the fastest manuscript typing in town and for being so moved by my draft that you cried into the keyboard.

Introduction

Quite a number of friends have looked worried when they discovered I was writing a book about heaven. The conversations have gone something like this:

'I hear you're writing a new book, Max.'

'That's right – I am writing about heaven.'

'Did you say heaven?'

'Yes, I said heaven.'

'Oh!'

There is often a pause here, there is almost embarrassment. If the book was about evangelism or church history it would be easier to know what to say next. I often have to help out at this point, 'Yes, I'm finding it really fascinating.'

'Good, good.' They are playing for time. I need to help out a bit more.

'Yes, I'm really excited about it. Looking forward to what it's going to be like makes a real impact on living now.'

'I see.' The puzzled look in their eyes tells me they don't see at all. So I know what's coming next. 'But how can you write a whole book about heaven – we really don't know much about it, do we?'

'I'm not so sure about that.' I am polite, so I don't

say 'rubbish'. 'Yes, there *is* quite a lot we don't know, but there's a whole lot we *do* know. And there is a great deal we can work out . . .'

This is not simply an academic quest for wider knowledge. Things we discover about God affect the way we live. I believe heaven is so wonderful that appreciating something more of its wonder could change our lives significantly. It certainly has made a deep impact on my life, since I started living in the light of heaven.

One thing seems clear to me if we are going to understand anything at all about heaven. We shall need to exercise our faith. However hard things may be to understand, or however odd some of the Bible's pictures of heaven may appear to be, we shall need to have a kind of willing faith which is motivated to find out more, but is also content to trust God for whatever may remain a mystery.

Part One

Why Isn't Heaven Very Real to Us?

1

How a Friesian Bull Introduced Me to Heaven

One day, when I was a young child growing up on our farm in Sussex, one of our bulls escaped. It gave me my first inkling as to how close everyday life is to death — and eternity. Back in those days I loved to run down to the farmyard to see what Dad was doing. I had to be careful. Huge tractors could roar round the corner of the yard, and even our herd of cattle making their way out to a field could have been a danger to a small boy. But above all, there were the bulls. Their pens had six-foot high brick walls, and the gates were solid timber structures, secured by big steel bolts top and bottom.

Victor and Vanguard were certainly magnificent creatures. One was a vast Friesian; the other was a Hereford and slightly smaller, but the way he snorted through the ring in his nose gave me no illusions about the truth of my father's warnings. My brother and I would occasionally peep through the cracks in the access hatch when Victor was chewing his hay only inches away. Fear would run down my spine at the sight of such massive, brooding power.

One time I had seen Jack, a farm-hand, carefully leading Victor with a long pole clipped through the bull's nose-ring. He appeared able to control the bull, but I could see fear in Jack's eyes. Another time Vanguard had been moved to a yard while his pen was cleaned. Taking a fancy to the luscious grass beyond, he had put his head down, shoved with his horns and, with a powerful upward movement of his neck, had tossed the five-barred gate over his shoulders and merrily charged into the green field.

Entering the farmyard that particular sunny morning, I did my usual rounds. The friendly calves licked my hand with their rough tongues. I popped into Dad's stables to admire his horses – but not to touch. I was then on my way to the lambing pens when I heard a hoarse shout from Jack. 'Look out! Victor's out of his pen!'

Instant panic seized me. I was alone, in the middle of a big stretch of concrete yard, and any second Victor would appear. I could hear a commotion from the bull-pen and Dad shouting. Far across the yard lay the disused row of pigsties. I ran like a rabbit, my little wellies splashing through the muck. I reached the first pigsty and dived in, scuttling on to cower in the darkness on some straw in a far corner. The shouting and commotion outside terrified me. Victor was loose. Had he seen me enter the pigsty? Would he come crashing through the little door? Feeling I was about to die, I sobbed hysterically.

When some time later Victor was recaptured, I crept out from the darkness of the pigsty. I could hardly believe that I was still alive. I was looking shakily over the railings when my Dad found me.

'You all right, old fella?' he asked, lifting me out of the pigsty, and glancing at my tear-stained face. Then he put an arm around me and said, 'You're quite safe, Victor is locked up now.' I sniffed and then to my great surprise he added, 'You will *always* be all right – you've asked Jesus into your heart, haven't you?'

I nodded, speechless. At this point my mother appeared and my Dad smiled and went back to work. As I stumbled back home for some hot chocolate with Mum, I was deep in thought. It was quite obvious my Dad associated faith in Jesus with total security and safety. That night I knelt beside my bed and asked Jesus again to be my friend and come into my heart. I had done it before, but I thought it wouldn't do any harm a second time – to make sure!

After that, the fact of God's love and the assurance of his care became very real to me. I have never seriously doubted since that I belonged to God and that heaven was a reality. I am not saying that they have always had the same sense of *nearness*. That has grown over the years. A lot of things are like that, aren't they? At school in my early teens 'A' levels seemed too far away to bother about. However, with 'O' levels behind us, I remember my biology teacher saying one day, 'Don't think you've got lots of time – every day counts. Those exams will be here before you know it.' Panic seized me. I resolved to do the very best I could. I passed my biology and chemistry with flying colours – which amazed my teachers – though I still failed physics. Things which seem far away creep up on you and all too soon become reality.

But how real is eternity to other people?

While researching this book, I asked various friends and acquaintances, 'Is heaven real to you and are you looking forward to being there?' The response varied enormously. Some responded with a huge smile and a deeply felt, 'Oh yes, very much so – and I can't wait!' Others gave me a shy grin or a serious quizzical look

7

and said, 'To be honest, I have really never thought about that.'

There was practically every sort of variation in between those two answers as well. Quite a few were cautiously optimistic, but couldn't really visualise how things would be. A frequent phrase that cropped up was, 'It sounds awful to say this, but I have this feeling it could be a bit boring.' Some even appeared quite content to put all these big questions on one side and just 'get on with life'. Others admitted that they live with the constant inner tension of not really knowing who they are or where their life is going.

I am not pretending this was any sort of scientifically conducted opinion poll. But the overwhelming majority of people I asked admitted that heaven was not very real to them and, as a natural consequence, they had no overwhelming eagerness to get there.

So why does eternity seem *so* far away to us?

Death by remote control

Life in today's Western world insulates us from some uncomfortable facts that would otherwise cause eternity to be more constantly in our thoughts. *The remoteness of death* is probably one of the strongest factors. In our society we are shielded even from the simple reality of *seeing* dead people. Oh yes, we may see horrific scenes on television, but we know the movies are all make-believe, and the tragic news in the headlines is almost always about things far away – it doesn't happen to *us*.

I am probably unusual in that I first saw a dead person when I was only twelve years old. I'd come home from school and gone into our 'back' kitchen, where all our boots were kept, as well as a big stack of logs for the sitting-room fire. As I turned to put my boots on the rack I noticed him. Crumpled in an unnatural position over his barrow full of logs was Charlie. He'd retired from heavy work on the farm some years ago, but still used to help my mother a few hours a week. Charlie was always very kind to me as a small boy. Now his muddy boots and old grey tweed jacket were strangely still, and a cold fear gripped me. I went over and put a hand on his shoulder, saying, 'Charlie, are you all right?' I thought that he must have fainted. The lack of response and the grey colour of his face told me things were more serious. The Charlie I'd known was no longer there, he had passed over into eternity. Seeing, touching, the dead body of an old friend was a milestone, and it affected me for weeks afterwards.

But how many people go through this experience? True, in the USA, it is normal practice to have the deceased on view in an open coffin. But the body is dressed in smart clothes, and make-up is used so that the face looks alive. You see a dead body, but every effort is made to prevent you thinking that the person is really dead.

The second fact Western society tries to shield us from is that *life is a constant risk*. As modern medicine pushes up life-expectancy figures we have less sense of our fragility and more confidence that we personally will live for years and years – well beyond the biblical 'three score years and ten'. This confidence doesn't even seem dented by the fact that most of us know someone who has died in a car accident, or whose days have been cut short by cancer. When I was sixteen, and at boarding-school, we boys were surprised to be told by the prefects one day that we had to assemble in the chapel just before dinner. No one knew why. As we filed in a very sombre-

9

looking headmaster stood at the front. When all three hundred boys had sat down in the rows of oak pews, the headmaster began:

'I have called you together to give you some very bad news. Michael Cahill was killed today in a car accident.' The usual fidgeting in the assembly instantly halted. The chapel was so quiet you could have heard a pin drop. Michael was a year older than I was, a high-spirited lad. He had broken the school rules by taking a car out. It was an understandable temptation for any mischievous boarding-school boy, but now he was dead. So final. He had crossed the line from time into eternity long before he had intended to and there was no way back. He was the first person of my age that I knew who was snatched from this life to the next. Eternity suddenly seemed very close again.

Yet, despite these reminders that life is always lived on a knife-edge, it is very easily possible for us to spend much of our lives untouched by death. We rarely face the reality that the statistics of those who die are one out of one. It is not 50 per cent of people who die. It is 100 per cent. This should not be some surprise that sneaks up on us. It is the only certain thing in the life of any living person. Yet even when people *do* die, they are referred to as having 'passed away' or 'gone to a better place'. We rarely refer to them as 'dead'.

Even when we are old we don't want to prepare ourselves for death. Sure, the solicitors urge us to make wills and to tidy our affairs for the benefit of the next of kin, but somehow openly discussing your coming death, and preparing for it, is not really acceptable. It is considered almost morbid. Death is seen as an unmitigated disaster, to be forestalled as long as possible, not the natural conclusion to any and all life here on earth.

How a Friesian Bull Introduced Me to Heaven

My brother and I were very close to our grandfather. He lived on the farm next door and we often rode our ponies through the woods to see him. He had driven me to school, tested me on my tables and was a permanent feature of life. One morning, when we were in our early teens, my Dad walked into our dining-room where we were breakfasting at the big carved oak table, and gripped the back of one of the tall chairs. Quietly he said, 'Grandpa Sinclair went to heaven during the night.' I don't remember him saying much more and I don't think we said anything at all. It was one of those moments when time stands still. My brother and I sat there, utterly stunned. Another milestone had been passed.

This grandpa who tested us on maths and would kick a football round the garden had also been a captain of industry. He had been managing director of a large public company. He had flown across the Atlantic during the war on secret negotiations and missions. He had been offered a knighthood but declined. He was wealthy enough to drive a Rolls Royce, but chose a Hillman. This grandpa was a hero not just to us, but in the world's eyes too. He had used his wealth to help others. He was a devout Christian who at one point in his life went out preaching every night after work and planted numerous new churches around the Tyneside area where he then lived. Now he was gone. That was sad, wrenching news. But Dad said he had gone to heaven and had utter confidence in this. The knowledge that Grandpa was at peace and safe with God for all eternity seemed good and fitting to me. It took away any horror of his death, and indeed seemed a fitting and natural conclusion to his life here on earth. At thirteen, heaven seemed near once again.

Glittering distractions

Another reason why the West wants to ignore death is that life has so much to offer – more this century than perhaps ever since the world began. And don't I know it, for I have recently been for a drive in a most beautiful car. A dream car. I was in Canada for a wedding. They were short of a driver for the wedding party, so I was volunteered. We drove to the Hertz Rental place in my cousin's well-worn Mazda truck. We couldn't really drive a bride and bridesmaids around in a thing like that – hence the rented cars. As we drove in, he pointed to a dazzling new white Lincoln Continental.

'Not that one!' I said incredulously, but a big grin spread across my face. I had always dreamed of driving a big American luxury car. I sank into the plush leather seating, surrounded by wood veneer. I gripped the cushioned steering-wheel, and stretched my feet on deep, thick-pile carpet. The whole car oozed luxury. I eased away from the kerb and what felt like hundreds of horsepower purred from the vast, powerful engine. My beautiful Lincoln Continental glided down the street and I was living out my fantasy.

We were soon on the freeway. At the push of a button I switched to cruise control. Then I discovered all sorts of other buttons. A gentle press and my seat would go forwards, backwards, up or down. Another button, and my back support could be increased or decreased. Another one, and the car suspension changed from the plush ride of a limousine to the hard firmness of a sports car. That car exceeded my wildest dreams. Unfortunately, I got to the church before I had a chance to try all the buttons.

For many men, luxury cars are a favourite daydream. Perhaps it doesn't happen to be your dream – but maybe there are other kinds of tangible experiences you would love to have, and in your daydreaming moments you run on and develop them. Something whispers that if you possessed X, Y or Z, it would add a permanent 'feel good' factor to your life. It would assure you that you had achieved something, been successful, fulfilled your true self. It would even lift you to a happier plane of existence.

Advertising encourages these kinds of dream. Everything from the clever television commercials to the cunning of a photographer's art in a magazine, persuades us to dream about things which are very earthbound. Homes, cars, boats, clothes, jewellery, exotic travel, sports, or even a whole *lifestyle* – and just about everything pushed at us on the television commercials has a pretty girl attached to ownership of the object. Advertisers subtly present material possessions as the key to enjoyment of life and love. We live in a world which acknowledges the truth of the Beatles' line 'money can't buy me love' but which doesn't really believe it. We wouldn't go on seeing these ads if they didn't work.

I guess you could think that most of these dreams are pretty harmless, but I would say that many are not. If I were to put myself in the devil's shoes and think how I was going to persuade people who have glimpsed something of the incredible value of eternal things, not to pursue them too hard; and those who have no clue about anything spiritual, not to *want* to get involved in anything spiritual, one of my strategies would certainly be to make the things of earth grow enormously large and bright, so that the light of God's love and his eternal values for living seemed rather small, dull and intangible. So is it any wonder that there is a shortage of eternal perspective?

Now there's absolutely nothing wrong with material

possessions in themselves – they are neutral things. If God blesses you with success and some of the toys that go with it, he has probably done so knowing he can trust you with it all, or allowing it to be a test of your stewardship, an opportunity for you to give the credit to God rather than take it yourself. But the big problem with dreams that are earthbound is that they take up space for dreaming about things not tied to planet earth. In fact, the Bible tells us very specifically how to fill our dreams. 'Fix your *mind* on things above . . . fix your *heart* on things above,' Paul tells us in Colossians 3:1–3. 'Let heaven fill your thoughts . . .'

I certainly need to check up on myself about this one. What do I daydream about? What are my mind and heart set on? If they are set on things on earth, this will affect my attitudes and priorities in life and sift down into my lifestyle. The man in the New Testament parable had worked long and hard to fill his barns full of good things. When he did that, he considered himself safe and successful, and decided he could relax, take things easy and enjoy all he'd ever dreamed about, because he'd made it. But God called him a fool because his time was up and he'd spent his limited lease investing in the wrong things.

The trouble is that earthbound things are so very *real*, aren't they? And I don't think there has ever been a time in history when in many places around the Western world anyone with initiative and hard work couldn't have a reasonable chance of expecting at least some of their earthbound dreams to come true. Only a generation or two ago this was impossible. You were born into a certain section in society, and no matter what you did you would never move out of it. I appreciate that the situation has not changed for millions of people around the world. But in many places the opportunities *are* there, and you don't have to be a Thatcherite to want to improve your lot and that of your family.

But the more we feed the dreams of glittering, worldly prizes, the less our starved spirits will be able to take to their wings and mature in preparation for the eternity they were made for. *'It could be you'*, smiles the clever lottery advertisement, persuading you against all logic to part with hard-earned money on the negligible chance that you might become very rich. The advertising man who came up with that one knew how to appeal to you and me. Dreams of a luxury lifestyle take some resisting.

Of course, you don't have to daydream about being a millionaire to allow the devil a foothold in your private inner self. Our lower worldly nature prefers anything it can see, touch or feel to anything intangible. Material possessions can be dangled in front of us, so that we take one little step forward (or spiritually speaking, backward) at a time. 'If I drove a car like that . . . if we lived in a home like this . . . if I was on the next rung of the promotion ladder . . . I would be happy.' Of course I am not making a virtue of poverty, but most of us are already materially rich by overall world standards. Even so, the devil makes sure that we keep on working at amassing more, with the false promise that 'then we shall be happier'.

As the evangelist, J. John, has said, 'We live in a society where we buy things we don't need with money we don't have to impress people we don't even like.' St Peter warns us in his letters that we can make some bad, bad mistakes in this area. All that we can see around us is *not* as solid and lasting as it looks. All that we cannot see around us is what *does* last.

To lead a life based on pursuing dreams that indulge

our selfishness ought to fail miserably with every Christian. Unfortunately, it doesn't always fail. It is quite possible to live a life that is in some ways Christian but, underneath it all, is based in this world. It is no wonder then that the ultimate realities are not very real to us, since a good deal of our energy, hearts and minds are spent elsewhere. 'You cannot serve both God and Mammon' (Matt. 6:24).

Fortunately we have a God who has power that no advertising money can buy and he has a route into everyone's heart.

Big ambitions – but are they big enough?

What are your greatest ambitions? Your answer will reveal a lot about where your dreams lie, and whether you have been hooked by Satan's earthbound strategy, or by God's wonderful offer of heaven. Our ambitions for what we can achieve in life can be a major distraction from facing spiritual realities.

On a flight from Sydney to Melbourne I found myself sitting next to a very smartly dressed young man in business suit and tie, and we got chatting. (On most plane journeys you can tell in the first thirty seconds whether your neighbour is happy to chat, or else sending out vibes which say, 'If you dare talk to me, I'll hit you with this newspaper.') He lived in Hong Kong and worked for a rapidly expanding company. After a few harmless preliminaries, I said, 'You must be very keen, travelling to your next appointment on a public holiday.'

'Yes, I am,' he replied with no smile. 'I work very hard.'

He was keen to talk and work was obviously a high

priority, so I ventured my key question. 'So, do you mind my asking, do you have some specific ambitions?'

'Oh yes, I have,' he came back without hesitation. 'I've been working for this company for two years now. I'm saving for a car. A year from now I'm going to buy it, a BMW.' He described the 700 Series model he would buy: it would be green with cream leather seats, and he listed a dozen other features it would have. 'That will impress my colleagues and also make a good impression with the directors. They like to see an executive who is not wasting his money, but can work towards a controlled target – not only at work but in handling his own affairs.'

'Well, that's a very specific ambition,' I ventured.

'That's the first step,' he continued, getting into his stride. 'I will be thirty-three when I buy the car and a year later I am going to get married. The company directors like a new director to be married and I aim to reach that level before I'm more than thirty-five.'

'That's step two,' I said, increasingly intrigued. 'You have certainly got your plans mapped out.'

'I aim to be managing director by the time I am forty,' he replied seriously. 'If I am not at that level by then, I shall either be headhunted, or be getting a job at that level with another company.'

I had listened intently throughout all this and he could see I took him seriously. 'If I may say so, you are very unusual,' I said. 'I'm not sure I've ever met someone with such very specific plans.'

'Perhaps you are right, but I want to live a certain lifestyle and I know this is the way to achieve it.' Cool, calculating, ambitious and earthbound, I thought. Then he came out with exactly what I hoped he'd say. 'Do you have ambitions?' he asked.

As the coffee arrived I grinned at him and silently

prayed, *Oh boy, do I have ambitions! Lord, help me right now*. 'Yes,' I said with a smile, 'my big one is to get to heaven and take as many people with me as possible.' (I borrowed that from charismatic leader John Wimber, but I didn't think he'd mind.)

'Oh!'

'I got my ticket to heaven when I was only a kid – it's a gift you see, you can't work at earning it. But now I am on a strategy which has two strands to it. First, I want to be exactly the kind of person my boss wants me to be – which affects every part of my life. Second, I am working hard each day in his business to try and persuade anyone I can that what he has to offer is the best thing since sliced bread – and more! As a matter of fact, I'm on my way now to speak to a hundred people at a dinner function.'

'You're going to make a speech?'

'Yes, I'll be the most persuasive I can. But it's sometimes hard because folk have never thought of anything as good as this before. It's tough, too, explaining that getting into God's family costs you nothing at all – it's a gift. But living the new life costs you everything. Yes, that's what I'm doing tonight.'

We sat there sipping our coffee and grinning at each other. Then he put his cup down and laughed. 'You're unusual – in a funny kind of way you're a bit like me!'

'You are right, but there's one big difference.' I hoped he'd take this one on the chin.

'What's that?' he asked.

'I'd say the difference is that if you are right and I am wrong, I don't think I would have lost anything living the way I do. But if I am right and you are wrong, I am going to go on living a very happy, contented life past this one into the next. And you are going to find you have made a terrible mistake because you will be in deep, deep trouble.'

I said this with a heavy heart because it was a heavy statement.

'That's logical,' he said. Dropping his guard completely, he went on to chat about his Catholic upbringing and the fact that because he had no real experience of anything spiritual he had turned to a life of serious material ambitions. 'And now that I'm well on my way I would have to go and sit next to you!'

The plane landed. I offered him a copy of a book I'd written. He shook my hand and thanked me for our conversation. Eternal realities can triumph over material ones, however real. I don't suppose I'll ever know whether Satan's schemes were frustrated in that young man's life as a result of our conversation that day. As I walked off the plane I certainly prayed that the Holy Spirit would illuminate the eternal and switch off some of the bright lights surrounding the temporal for Mike. He was making a terrible mistake with his life and had fallen into the trap the devil laid for him. God bless Mike wherever he is today.

2

Why Do We Think Like We Do?

It is not just the alluring pull of material things which makes the eternal less real. We live in an age which has 'progressed' over the last century or so from broadly Christian beliefs and values to a secularism unparalleled in world history. We question everything our ancestors held sacred for centuries. The only thing we don't question is whether or not we are *right* to question – and doubt – everything. To understand why we are now so unsure about what to believe, we need to see how this major shift in thinking came about.

For most of the history of Western Europe, people were happy to accept three great truths. First, we knew about things because God had revealed them to us. Second, God was involved and relevant to every aspect of our being and lives. Third, there was life after death, and what we did in this life affected where we went after we died. Not even the Renaissance and the Reformation shattered this consensus. People might express and visualise how God impacted on their lives very differently (contrast Dutch and Italian art of the early seventeenth century), but they did not doubt the fact that he did.

The real sea-change in thinking came as the spiritual passions of the Reformation and the Counter-Reformation began to cool. And it started with men like Descartes (1598–1650). Descartes believed in God, but he also was searching for a more rational basis to understand the universe. He therefore resolved 'never to accept anything as true' if he did not have 'evident knowledge of its truth'. He had in fact shifted the starting place for the search for truth from God to man.

Subsequent generations of thinkers adapted and developed the thinking of men like Descartes, so that by the mid- to late-eighteenth century 'reason', not God, was generally accepted as the starting point for discovery about life. The philosophers of that time, such as Voltaire and Rousseau, saw the answers to the ignorance, superstition and injustices of their society as coming from the increase of human knowledge and the application of rational principles. God, eternity, faith; these were concepts which they didn't think could be verified, so were irrelevant to real life.

These ideas grew in popularity during the nineteenth century. It was true that religion was still valued in Victorian England, but increasingly its relevance was seen as limited to morals, outward conduct and manners. Of the great truths of the past only the idea of an after-life still seemed important, but even this became more vague in people's minds as the other principles about God's involvement in our world were increasingly eroded. Science and human progress would enable us to deal with man's problems. Utopia now became the vision, built in England's green and pleasant land by man's own hands. People slowly ceased to live with 'one eye on eternity'. (David Winter, *Hereafter*, Hodder, 1972).

So strong did people's faith in science grow that when, erroneously, they began to sense that science and Christianity were in final conflict (e.g. in Darwin's theory of evolution, or in liberal research over the accuracy of the Bible), they assumed science was right and faith was undermined. It was the First World War that finally shattered people's confidence that human, scientific progress was the answer. For it was the very weapons science had created – the machine-gun, the high explosive shell, the Zeppelin, the submarine – that magnified the horror of war. Rational justification for the slaughter was advanced by all sides, but hard to accept.

Throughout this century, we have never really recovered our confidence in rational or scientific solutions to life. We have rejected the answers put forward by the thinkers of past generations as flawed, yet we still assume that in their dismissal of God as irrelevant to life they were right.

The disillusionment that the First World War caused resulted in a profound change in the mood of young people. A whole generation of young men had been photographed smiling in their new uniforms – and then marched off to the killing fields of France. Few returned – and they were no longer smiling. A mood of immense disillusionment and frustration over the futility of war spread through a generation. Eloquent poems such as those by Rupert Brooke expressed the feelings of the day.

Hardly a family in the British Isles remained unaffected. We weren't. A stone memorial in Theipval, France, carries the name, Harold Sinclair – my great-uncle, one of some 100,000 men missing in action and never found. He was one of those smiling young men in uniform, when he left his home in Hexham, Northumberland.

God raised up Christians to provide the message that was desperately needed for that hour. Amongst them was a writer, Paterson Smyth. In the midst of his grieving and war-scarred generation he wrote *The Gospel of the*

Hereafter. He described it in this way: 'This book is a poor, imperfect attempt to put together some of the teachings of our holy religion, to help a troubled world, in a day of its necessity, to look out over the wall.' The need of his day was so obvious – to be able to face death and to have hope beyond the grave.

Right up to the late 1950s many people felt God was still important as far as life *after* death was concerned. Most people still paid lip-service to Christian morality while not understanding, or even believing, in the fundamental truths that underpinned it. God was still useful as a last resort; someone you could turn to if everything else failed.

This was the society in which I grew up. It still believed that life had a meaning, and continued after death. Heaven was real, and the vast majority of people you spoke to would tell you they would like to get there. (Even those who added, 'but I'm not very good, so I probably won't.') That kind of hope was probably not well defined and not much of it was genuine Christian faith. But it was there as the base-line of many people's thinking.

Certainly many people held sub-Christian sentimental beliefs in life after death being peaceful, as they still do today. Someone I met recently had just lost her mother. 'Well, I suppose at least she is at peace now,' was the sad conclusion. After a long and painful illness it was all over, and surely the latter situation had to be better than the former.

People say these kinds of things to cope with death. The sentiments expressed may not be based on any firm grounding, but they show how impossible it is for us to accept that a much-loved personality can be just snuffed out. Something intuitive tells us that personality is too valuable to push off the end of a precipice and be lost forever. Something must go on. Somehow, somewhere, we will be reunited again. There may be vague, misty Christian ideas at the back of this belief, but sadly there are at least a couple of errors in it, and the Bible shows up its shortcomings.

For one thing, my friend seemed to have no awareness of the fact of judgment. Not everyone goes to heaven. That doesn't seem to be a very nice thing to say and because we don't regard it as acceptable to criticise the dead, it is almost as if we expect God to respect the same convention.

The other flaw is the notion that the next life will be very much a straightforward continuation of this one; that it will simply be 'part two' of the serial. To quote David Winter again: 'The truth is so much more convincing and so much more glorious that it is sad to see simple faith satisfied with rather tawdry imitations of the real thing.'

But gradually even these sentiments too have been questioned, and quite logically. If you no longer accept a Christian God, why live by his precepts – or his promise of heaven?

I love to go swimming at a gorgeous open-air pool quite near our home. During the summer, my wife Sue and I sometimes meet other early-morning enthusiasts. Amongst them is an older lady. Like me, she has a disability and hobbles to the water's edge with her walking stick. I cheerfully greeted her early one morning and enquired after her health.

'Oh, I'm not too bad I suppose,' she replied. 'But I guess I'm getting rather old and creaky.'

'Well, I'm creaky too,' I agreed. 'I really am looking forward to heaven and getting a new pair of legs,' I added for good measure. She is a very sweet-natured soul, so her reaction to this remark startled me. A look of something approaching horror flooded her face. 'I'm not at all sure about that,' she retorted. 'I'm not expecting more after this!'

Something inside of me shrivelled up. It so saddened me to think that the eternal hope which God had originally caused this lady to be born with had somewhere over the years been strangled to death. As of course it has for millions of people since the First World War. Many since then have asked: what guiding light *are* we to live by?

In the decades that have rolled by since then, we have unwittingly, step by step, thrown the constituent parts of hope overboard. It all began as a quest for rational, objective 'truth' and 'meaning' so that the boat would sail more smoothly without excess baggage on board. But the end result appears to be that we have thrown the anchor and the rudder overboard too.

However, many of the writers and philosophers who led the attack on hope and meaning, such as Rousseau, Nietzsche and the Marquis de Sade, could not be said to have had great integrity. Perhaps their attacks on Christian belief have not so much been a quest for truth as a desire to be freed from moral constraint. Their personal lives do not bear much examination or evoke great admiration.

Yet the insidious philosophy which plants doubts in our minds as to whether we can really ever know anything, and whether we can really ever communicate with one another, sinks deep into our consciousness. It pervades much of what we read and see. It may reinforce the idea that only what I am experiencing now, *this second*, is valid. It may convince me that my feelings and experiences are much more important than struggling with ideas and words which may not mean anything at all.

The devil has used this subjective reasoning to very good effect. Complete confusion reigns in the minds of many people, and of course its logical end is a total despair. It undermines the basic human need to love and be loved, because I can never know if what I think is love really is. I am therefore robbed of that wonderful warm sense of security, which is everyone's birthright.

More important than that, we are robbed of the certainty of knowing life itself by knowing God. All is put into question and we become unsure as to whether we can know anything at all. And the uncertainty is doubly uncertain about things that cannot be seen. If there are questions about whether we are really communicating with people our physical eyes can see and touch, how much more will we tend to question those unseen realities we cannot see and touch – God, eternity and heaven?

The sixties saw another major attack on the remnant of Christian values that were still imprinted on our society. This teenage generation was the first in decades not to grow up under the shadow of world war or economic depression and it was determined to make a bright new start. This has been the vision of many generations in the past, but the sixties youth culture decided that it could only be achieved by revolution, and not evolution. All the values and beliefs of their parents were up for grabs and the underlying assumption was that anything old must be obsolete. 'Rules and regulations, who needs them. Throw them out the door,' sang Crosby, Stills and Nash. It was the time of the sexual revolution and the first mass drug culture. Nothing was sacred. 'Imagine there's no heaven, it's easy if you try,' sang John Lennon.

It was a time of massive optimism, yet in removing so many of the final anchoring points in the established social structures, this generation was condemning future generations to drift, unless they provided a better alternative.

And that indeed has been the story of the following

decades, as new generations have sought to establish some new framework in which to belong. And they have felt compelled to do so without looking to the past or the future.

The seventies saw a search for security in image. Outrageous outfits, customised Ford Capris and an ever-changing identikit, as punk replaced glitter, only in turn to be superseded by neo-romanticism. The eighties saw the search switch back to materialism as the answer. Greed was suddenly good for you and for the national economy. New Age became a mainstream philosophy as the designer faith which enabled you to take what suited you, and didn't conflict with your materialistic goals. No wonder it grew in popularity.

And now, at the turn of the millennium, the optimism of the 1960s is long gone, and there seems a marked absence of hope. The suicide rate has increased dramatically and most live to escape the reality of life. We escape on exotic holidays, or to theme parks (the artificial is far more reassuring than the natural as we remain in control), virtual reality, or the clubbing scene. We endure our 'manic Mondays' so we can live for our 'fun days'. But escapism is a sure sign of the absence of hope in our society, and the unwillingness to face reality is a growing malaise.

There is no doubt that the last half century has seen the disappearance of a great deal of hope, meaning and direction in people's lives. Along with it has gone the hope of heaven. Bertrand Russell summed up the unspoken feelings of many people: 'There is darkness without, and when I die there will be darkness within. There is no splendour, no vastness anywhere; only triviality for a moment and then nothing.'

The equipment does not seem to have been left

around which enables people to choose what David Winter describes as: 'Either a noble humanism that faces death as the final extinction of a life well lived, or a true Christianity which looks on and beyond to a life with God.'

At present most of us in the West are not faced with death – we are faced with life. But because we have no certainty about God's wonderful plans for us beyond this life, we have no certainty about life itself. If you have nothing worth dying for, you have nothing worth living for. Uncertainty about death leads to insecurity about life. So we cling desperately to life, prolong it by any means, and give priority to any procedure, method or research which may make it last longer. If it's all we've got, there is every reason to be desperate. A friend of mine said to me recently, 'I am determined to enjoy every minute of my life while I have it, because when I die that's it, that's the end.' He is an eloquent representative of a considerable number of people – especially men – who subscribe to the 'this life is all there is' view.

To dull our brains and numb the senses against our predicament, we snatch at anything that will distract us or provide a little pleasure. Each chooses according to their taste. Some choices are socially acceptable – career success, sport, drinking alcohol, taking prescribed anti-depressants. Some are generally frowned on – injecting, sniffing, swallowing or smoking drugs. But the Bible tells us that man was created as a spiritual being. We are made in the image of God. We long for a God-like dimension to our lives. And therefore it's not surprising to find that modern man, being led to a point of despair by liberal thinkers, looks in what he thinks is a new direction for some deeper ingredient to life.

Modern man has accepted the lie that Christianity, after

two thousand years, has been discredited. With the new millennium approaching, the idea of a new era with new kinds of spiritual values is appealing.

Eternity, yes, but is it heaven?

Not everyone is an ardent materialist, by any means. Not all avoid the idea of death and eternity. Some look up, as I did one night in Australia.

I first visited Australia way back in 1987. Several people who had read my books invited me down under on a speaking and ministry tour. It was a memorable three weeks. The tour was based on the major cities of Australia: enjoyable, but I really longed to see some of the country's spectacular scenery. I finally managed it on my seventh trip, when a group of Baptist churches invited me to a series of missions in the Kimberley and Pilbarra region of the vastness of north-west Australia. I stayed a few days in a little town called Karratha in the home of Arthur and Jane Payne.

One night, Arthur said, 'Do you want to see something to lift your soul?' We hopped into his Land Rover and drove a few miles out of town – and were into open bush. Arthur stopped the car and the heavy stillness of the warm night surrounded us. A gentle slope hid the town from us so that it seemed as if we were surrounded by thousands of miles of uninhabited Australia. Arthur leaned across the bonnet of the Land Rover and quite simply said, 'Now turn your eyes heavenwards and have a good look.' I did, and it certainly lifted the soul.

Being in the southern hemisphere and away from any other lights, the star scene was absolutely spectacular. The brighter stars blazed like lanterns, a dazzling sight, while the lesser stars glittered and sparkled. Even little patches of light which are actually whole clusters of stars on the outer edges of our galaxy glowed like a dense white mist. Our own galaxy has around eight thousand million stars and planets. Beyond our galaxy are thousands more, with millions of stars. We were looking up into infinity. We eventually got back into the Land Rover and drove home in silence.

This exercise was certainly good for the soul. Something inside of me spends a lot of time telling me that I am the centre of the universe. A few billion stars above me is an excellent reminder that I am really only a tiny speck on a tiny planet – and for a very short time at that. The immensity of outer space can crack open our narrow prospective and make it a little easier to begin thinking about eternity.

Of course, people have looked at the stars and thought about eternity for centuries. They have suspected that there is an after-life, and have built vast tombs and pyramids to honour their dead and prepare them for the next world. It seems to me that the vacuum created in recent decades by Western society's 'loss' of the Christian heaven has enabled all sorts of alternative ideas to be offered again.

It always amazes me that, despite rejecting Christianity, people will believe in almost anything else that provides a hint of something not purely material. In some circles it would be implied that we are now too sophisticated to believe the simple dogmas of Christianity, but many of the same people seem to be fascinated by their horoscopes in mass circulation magazines, and the dark and gloomy world of mystic ley lines and yin and yang.

Popular New Age thinking sees the answer as lying within us. All we need to do is free or release the potential within truly to find the fulfilment we seek. It leaves us in control of our destiny and free to explore our own freedom.

Interest in Eastern religions is also widespread, with their teaching that in some mysterious way the human personality can survive the end of physical life, and that perhaps some kind of immortal soul continues. The idea of reincarnation is now more widely accepted. I am sure you have heard people say: 'I think I came to this place in a former life.' The description of Nirvana by Buddha appeals to other people: 'Neither a coming nor a going, nor a standing still, nor a falling away, nor a rising up; but it is without fixity, without mobility, without basis.' That might be quite appealing if you are so fed up with life, living and conscious existence you wish it would all stop. Then Buddha's final sentence adds the final touch you are looking for: 'It is the cessation of becoming.'

You could truthfully say there is fascination with almost anything supernatural, from aliens and UFOs to occult and paranormal happenings. You name it; someone's following it. This is reflected in the popularity of films which deal with such subjects. Since television and movies so significantly shape people's values, whatever is portrayed on screen will be highly influential. The devil has managed a very neat takeover in these prime areas. How many movies have you seen recently which depict a Christian understanding of the spiritual world and heaven? How many have you seen which give alternative supernatural views? 'Near death' or 'out of body' experiences abound in television documentaries. Witches, werewolves and supernatural themes form the staple diet of children's television programmes. Millions follow the adventures of agents Mulder and Scully in *The X Files* has a phenomenal following.

By contrast, aliens and UFOs were not a part of the thinking of one man who had more reason than most to think about life in outer space: the former astronaut, Colonel James Urwin. I met him in 1981, when it was my privilege to interview him on stage before a packed Albert Hall in London. As a child, he told us, he had looked out of his bedroom window up into the clear sky one night with his mother. 'I'd like to go there someday,' he'd said, pointing to the moon. As he grew up, flying became his obsession. His ambition was to fly higher and faster than any man on earth. He broke all kinds of flying records. An accident in a light aeroplane left him in a bad way. Typically, he fought back and it had to be something of a miracle that he was eventually chosen for the Apollo space programme.

I asked him if his trip to the moon had made him think of spiritual realities. 'It certainly did. I came back from the moon a different man. Seeing the earth like a tiny blue marble in space made me feel very small. It gave me a little bit more idea of eternity.'

Walking on the surface of the moon would have made many men very proud, but this man's glimpse of the eternity of space had had a very different effect on him. It deepened his Christian faith, and 'made me realise that Jesus's walk on earth was far more important than any man walking on the moon'.

I found it heartening to meet James Urwin, whose scientific background and personal experience of the hugeness of the universe, caused him to believe rather than doubt the Christian view of eternity. There are many others like him. But if Jesus's life and words are so important, and top scientists have no trouble in reconciling the truth of modern science with the truth of Christian revelation, why don't we hear more of this shouted loud and clear from the roof-tops by our churches? I believe there are reasons. I found it both a shock and a challenge to investigate them.

3

Too Earthly Minded to Be of
Any Heavenly Use?

Why isn't heaven more real to the Church? Many people
have told me they have never heard a sermon on heaven.
They may have gone to church for years, but they have
not been informed what the Bible really teaches on the
subject.

Some of today's churchgoers may hear more about
heaven from the media than the pulpit. Stories about
vicars and church leaders disagreeing on the theological
conundrums of heaven and occasionally denying the
existence of any sort of heaven or hell (or both), still
seem bizarre enough to news editors to make headlines. Confusion abounds for, while literal ideas of a
geographical heaven or hell don't seem to be currently
favoured by the Church, nobody has suggested anything
as an alternative.

I think the truth is that the Church has largely lost its
sense of the imminence of eternity – and 'after death, the
judgment'. The urgency of the gospel, with its clarion call
to people to wake from their sinful lives, seek forgiveness
and healing in Christ, is not a regular feature across the
spectrum of today's Church. Enthusiasm or urgency in
spiritual matters is seen by some as tasteless, extreme,

eccentric. Gentle politeness and understatement are seen to be so much more acceptable.

This loss of the sense of eternity has had drastic repercussions on today's Church. It shows immediately in a decreased priority for reaching out to unchurched people. It is reflected in the way many churches set their budgets and in what they consider to be important activities. How many church congregations across our country really believe that they are going to heaven and that their friends and neighbours who don't know Christ are not going there?

At the very least, the spirit of 'for me to live is Christ' could be said to be somewhat patchy across the map of the Church today. We contrast badly with the fervour people give to other causes. Often they are literally prepared to give their lives for what they believe in. IRA bombers risk everything – and sometimes lose it all. Palestinians will give their lives in suicide car bombs to protest against Israeli oppression. Perhaps the most striking example was fifty years ago. Japanese kamikaze pilots volunteered to fly suicide bombing missions against the American fleet. There was no persuasion, no pressure. Hundreds of young men offered to give their lives in the service of their emperor. A temporal cause, and a failed last-ditch attempt at that.

But when the Church is called to an eternal purpose, to give our lives for a ruler who is assured of final victory, where are we? Well-meaning, but distracted by the seduction of all that is around us? Of course, I'm not simply blaming 'the Church' – we are the Church! So we probably need to give ourselves a spiritual MOT.

For example, let's imagine a national survey of church members' finances. What would it show up? Suppose we analysed incomes and the average percentage of that given to church work, missions and evangelism. Suppose we looked at the percentage of income spent on entertainment or cars or extras – luxury items as opposed to necessities. Money talks and it would tell a story.

Suppose we also analysed time, the total time we have available. What percentage of that time do we spend in engaging in sharing our faith or sharing God's love with our neighbours? How much time do we set aside to grow in our faith, through church worship, prayer, Bible study and reading of Christian books? Compare that with the time we spend watching television and entertaining ourselves in various ways.

I am not trying to knock the legitimate need we have for relaxation, keeping fit, eating healthily and meeting people. There are a whole lot of perfectly normal activities in which we need to engage in life which are not specifically 'spiritual'. What I *am* getting at is that where we have choices to make about the way we spend our money, time and energy, those are the areas which show up our real beliefs. It is in these areas where our hunger for eternity and heaven will show if we have it.

Why was heaven more real to the very first believers?

It is a strange anomaly that living in times in which it is easier to serve God does not necessarily seem to be an advantage. One might think that having more money, better health, greater security and easier circumstances would encourage us all to walk more closely with God. But it seems instead that physical extremities develop greater spiritual depths in us. This leaves me wondering whether the hardships faced by former generations of believers (and many today) actually helped to highlight their sense of a reality beyond earth – the hope of heaven.

Look at the Old Testament, to begin with. The world was a harsher, more brutal place with suffering and injustice everywhere, and no Red Cross or European Court of Justice to take up your cause. So when men and women decided to turn their backs on the pagan cults and worship Yahweh, they were well aware that he really would be all they had in the world.

Think of Noah's dependence on God. There he was building an ark on dry ground, in full view of his cynical, mocking neighbours. But he looked beyond, believing the warning from the Lord about the flood and trusting him to save him. Think of Abraham and Sarah, leaving their secure homeland to wander in the wilderness, believing Yahweh's promise that they were the start of a great nation, but unable to have even one child – until the Lord worked a miracle and Sarah conceived Isaac. Again, they based their actions on their faith in God's promises. Think of Moses' terror at the idea of leading the Israelites out of Egypt. He knew the fledgling Israelite nation was an accident just looking for a place to happen. Without God the Israelites would have died by the Red Sea. Then think of the shepherd boy, David, who was told that he would be a great king. He was forced into hiding, and had to fling himself on God's mercy because Saul's soldiers were seeking to kill him, not crown him.

There are a few verses in Hebrews which hit the nail right on the head:

All these people were still living by faith when they died . . . and they admitted that they were aliens and strangers on earth. People who say such things show that they are looking for a country of their own. If

37

they had been thinking of the country they had left, they would have had opportunity to return. Instead, they were longing for a better country – a heavenly one. Therefore, God is not ashamed to be called their God, for he has prepared a city for them. (Heb. 11:13–16)

So what did these people have that made their 'heavenly country' so real to them? Faith. And with it, the commitment to live in the light of their faith, whatever that involved. Back to Hebrews. Chapter 12 opens with a pep talk, encouraging us to see the logical course of action we must take in view of what we have read in Chapter 11:

Since we are surrounded by such a great cloud of witnesses, let us throw off everything that hinders and the sin that so easily entangles, and let us run with perseverance the race marked out for us. (Heb. 12:1)

So there I am in a huge stadium, all set to compete in the long-awaited and prestigious athletics competition. There is a huge crowd looking on and taking great interest in my particular race. The interesting thing is that they are not just spectators; they have all competed in the same race some years back. So for me, they are inspiring examples, because they all did pretty well in the race. They know the secret of how to do well. Of course, it's not just me – you are competing as well.

Surrounded by these inspiring examples, let's get on with the job. There are four key factors we had better concentrate on. First, throw off everything that hinders a swift run – any unnecessary baggage certainly can't be taken along. Second, make sure there is nothing around that may trip you up – a significant number of runners take a fall and never finish. Third, be prepared for a long tough race – no one gets to the finish by accident and a lot of people drop out because it is tough. Fourth, stick to the race track marked out for you – there's all kinds of other places you could run, but you would be wasting your energy.

Maybe it is not quite so surprising that the very first believers had a better sense of a 'heavenly country' they were heading for.

Fired with excitement

When we come to the New Testament, we find God granting us significant new revelations about heaven. For a start, Jesus made some clear and personal promises in teaching his disciples. At a time when Jesus warns his disciples he is about to leave them, a very revealing conversation takes place. To paraphrase St John's Gospel:

Peter asks, 'Lord, where are you going?'

Jesus replies, 'Where I am going you cannot follow now, but you will follow later.' This obviously produced a number of puzzled or panic-stricken looks on disciples' faces, so the conversation continues.

Jesus says, 'Do not let your hearts be troubled.'

'Not troubled? You are going to leave us and you think we shouldn't be troubled. What do you expect us to do?'

'Trust in God; trust also in me.'

'Okay. But it really would help if we knew where you were going and why you are leaving us.'

'In my Father's house are many rooms. I am going there to prepare a place for you.'

'That's good news. But the only place we would ever want to be is where you are. So will we see you there?'

'If I go and prepare a place for you, I will come back and take you to be with me.'

No, Jesus did not tell them everything – but he did make some very specific promises. And that must have made heaven real to them (John 13 and 14). These kinds of promises about the future were probably not what anyone was expecting. The Jews were looking for a more earthbound Messiah, who would liberate their occupied country. Their daydreams were filled with visions of parades displaying massive military might, and the restoration of their country's independence as a sovereign state. So Jesus's statement to Pilate was not a politically correct one for the Jews of his day: 'My kingdom is not of this world. If it were, my servants would fight . . . but now my kingdom is from another place' (John 19:36).

Even so, with Jesus's death, the disciples lost their vision for a while, and hid behind closed doors. It was seeing their leader rise from the dead that galvanised them. The resurrection and the ascension gave the disciples their first real inkling as to the wonderful future that awaited them.

Notice how in Jesus's appearances after his resurrection he stresses the heavenly kingdom, and 'I go to my father.' The disciples' relationship with Jesus was the crux on which all else rested. 'If you abide in me and I in you . . . then my Father and I will abide with you' and out of this, heaven follows naturally.

Then, with the sending of the Holy Spirit, as told at the start of Acts, the early Christians suddenly gained their confidence. They were fired with great excitement. The persecutions of early Christians must have given a rather different meaning to evangelistic sermons. If you heard Paul preach about 'the cost of being a Christian', you would have known what it meant. It certainly was costly. Paul had both meted out persecution and also experienced it. He had seen Stephen sink to his knees as boulders rained down on him from furious Jews. Did the cost destroy Stephen's faith? No! He's the one who cried: 'I see heaven open and the Son of Man standing at the right hand of God' (Acts 7:56). Not the words of one in despair, but in triumph. The tough times made heaven very real for Stephen, certainly just before he stepped across the threshold and arrived there. These early Christians were galvanised by the realisation that they were in reality members of a different kingdom, and that they would be reunited with Christ.

And then, of course, the great apostle, Paul. His faith still echoes down the centuries, two thousand years on. But at the time it meant to him the loss of all earthly things. Why did it not matter? Why was eternity and heaven so real to him? With these thoughts going round in my head I went to my study, opened my NIV Study Bible and put the question to Paul. He gave me a pretty definite answer:

For me, to live is Christ and to die is gain. If I am to go on living in the body, this will mean fruitful labour for me. Yet what shall I choose? I do not know! I am torn between the two: I desire to depart and to be with Christ, which is better by far; but it is more necessary for you that I remain in the body. Convinced of this, I know that I will remain, and I will continue with all of you for your progress and joy in the faith, so that through my being with you again your joy in Christ Jesus will overflow on account of me. (Phil. 1:21–26)

41

I looked out of the study window to our garden bathed in bright morning winter sunshine and thought of Paul sitting in his study writing his letter, nearly two thousand years ago. It was probably during his house arrest in Rome, when he was free to talk to visitors and write letters. This one was a thank-you letter for a gift. As part of his normal thinking, he is writing to his fellow Christians expressing spontaneous enthusiasm at the idea of going to heaven and being with Christ. He is in no doubt that this is a million times better than sticking around on earth, but that puts him in a quandary. God has got a job for him here, and he obviously does not sense the green light to leave it. So reluctantly he reckons that he will stay. Not for his own benefit, but for the benefit of others and their 'progress and joy in the faith'.

Paul knew quite a lot about the occupational hazard of being a Christian. He had been shipwrecked several times, rejected as a turncoat by the Jews, flogged and imprisoned. As you read his biography in the book of Acts, there was hardly a town he went to where he left of his own accord. But in these conditions, which most of us Christians today would dread, he found the fertile seedbed not only to trust God for this life, but to see into the realities of the next. 'Caught up to the third heaven,' is how he describes it. 'Caught up to paradise' and hearing 'inexpressible things, things that human beings are not permitted to tell'.

So why are we so different? Why do most Christians today not have heaven very much in their thoughts? Part of the reason has to be in the depth of our commitment compared to Paul's. Can I say that, for me, to live is Christ? Can you say it?

I sometimes wonder whether some Christians I meet were motivated to invest in God's kingdom primarily for what they could get out of it by way of dividends. Don't misunderstand me – there are unbelievable benefits in this life from truly being a child of God. What price can you possibly put on the peace of mind which comes from knowing that you are known by God, loved, understood and forgiven? But these benefits were bought at a heavy price. Jesus Christ gave his life. We are invited to follow him in identifying with his death. 'We were therefore buried with him through baptism into death' (Rom. 6:4). I am therefore as good as dead and have started a new life. 'I have been crucified with Christ and I no longer live, but Christ lives in me' (Gal. 2:20). And that obviously has to have a radical effect on our new lives as Christians.

> Since you became alive again, so to speak, when Christ arose from the dead, now set your sights on the rich treasures and joys of heaven . . . you should have as little desire for this world as a dead person does. Your real life is in heaven with Christ and God.' (Col. 3:1, 3 Living Bible)

So this is why Paul feels as he does. His whole reason for living is to serve Christ and to serve others. He is living for things that last for eternity and therefore he can truthfully say that to die is gain.

How does today's Church look when you examine it in this light? What makes it so uncomfortable is that there is no checklist of items to tick, and if you get more than a certain percentage you are okay. Rather, this is a blanket appraisal which covers the depths of our *motivation*. It is about whether we are being obedient to Christ, the one who 'humbled himself and became obedient to death' (Phil. 2:8).

Whether we really believe our beliefs shows up in how

we live. The poster that was around a while back certainly brought me up with a start. 'If you were arrested and tried on the charge of being a Christian, would there be enough evidence to convict you?' There was plenty of evidence to convict Paul! His life was dominated by an enthusiasm for eternal realities. How do you and I measure up in comparison?

I feel that many times I have offered a gospel which heavily emphasised the benefits and played down the cost. I've been afraid that I might put people off because they would see a negative picture of things they would have to give up. I have sometimes hardly mentioned surrender and obedience, let alone explained them.

Maybe it's a bit like getting married. I know I dreamed only of the glorious joy of sharing my life with Sue twenty-four hours a day. It didn't dawn on me that there would be times when I would need to bite my lip and surrender what I wanted to what she wanted. That was why our first quarrel was such a surprise. It was over something really important: what colour to paint our bathroom. Our family bathroom in the farmhouse had been cream, so I knew that was the right colour for bathrooms. Sue's home had had a blue one, so of course I knew they had been wrong. Oddly, Sue did not see this. When the dust had settled, and our bathroom had been painted with a colour which neither of us liked, we both realised that sharing our lives wasn't going to be all easy. To 'submit to one another out of reverence for Christ' (Eph. 5:21) was going to require something of me to die inside. The prize was that something infinitely more precious and joyful would be born out of this.

To live for Christ means to die to what I want. But it is infinitely worthwhile. And the end result of it all, as Paul says, is that ultimately to die is gain.

Being helped into heaven by Nero and the rest

A sabbatical year recently gave me the opportunity to study some church history. I came away with a staggering picture of the dangers and suffering which the early Christians experienced. The Roman Emperor Nero lit the driveway to his palace with lampposts consisting of Christians strapped to poles covered in tar and set alight. Thousands of Roman citizens turned out for a Saturday evening's entertainment to see Christians forced to walk into an arena full of lions or gladiators.

There are some notable true stories. One of my favourite ancient ones would have to be Polycarp, Bishop of Smyrna (Izmir in modern Turkey). He was on trial for his life before a Roman governor for being a Christian. A man in his situation is shown up for what he really is.

To paraphrase what happened: the Roman governor invites Polycarp to renounce his faith so that he can be released and live a normal, peaceful life. The bishop asks the governor how he could possibly renounce the One whom he has served all his life. The governor threatens to take away his property. The bishop replies that he owns nothing – it all belongs to his master. The governor indicates he could keep him in prison for life. Polycarp replies that he would still be free. The governor threatens not only prison but solitary confinement. Polycarp points out that he would in reality never be alone.

Having threatened all that a man normally holds dear, the governor uses what he thinks is his trump card. 'Very well then, I will take away your life.' The bishop indicates where every day of his life has been invested by responding, 'Governor, proceed,' and explains that he will then live forever. Other Christians showed the same courage under those early Roman persecutions.

Not until the Emperor Constantine was himself converted, and Christianity became thereby 'respectable', did new dangers threaten the Church: complacency and shallow commitment. This caused a lot of concern in the early fourth century, especially among the Donatists of north Africa, who said anyone not wholly committed should be thrown out of the Church. But who is to say who truly believes? Only God can really know the heart of a person. To start such a 'witch hunt' would have led to endless splintering and schisms, and torn the Church apart from within.

In response to the crisis, the great 'father' of Western Christianity, Augustine, Bishop of Hippo, developed the doctrine of the 'invisible Church' within the visible, worldwide Church. He acknowledged that unfortunately, yes, not everyone who paid lip-service to Christ was a true believer, but that it was not up to people to judge and throw people out of the Church. There were true believers, and there were false believers, and both were known by God, and both were within the visible Church. In Augustine's great work, *The City of God*, he argued that the world is made up of 'two cities' or groups of people. Those who believed in Christ were citizens of the city of heaven. Those who did not, who believed in earthly powers, were bound for hell.

Augustine's teaching came at a critical time for the Church. The barbarians had overrun Rome in 410, and everywhere people felt it was the end of civilisation – that the worst possible of all things had happened. Augustine gave a priceless gift to the Church so hard pressed: a perspective of history that was spiritual. It was as if he said, 'Well, so what if Rome has fallen? With the coming of Christ, his death and resurrection, what does it matter? Temporal kingdoms *will* rise and fall, but that is

46

not the point of life. People should look beyond – to the spiritual realities of the kingdom of God.' Augustine's certainty as to the existence of the heavenly kingdom even when his city of Hippo was surrounded and taken was a great comfort to Christendom. As the Dark Ages closed over the people, this perspective of Christianity and eternity was to protect and nurture the Church for the next several centuries. From this, out of such dark times, it found the energy to engage in missionary outreach, for by the sixth century missionaries such as Patrick and Augustine and Columba were on the move . . . and out to conquer Ireland and England, not for any kingdom on earth, but for building a people for heaven.

Against such a 'cloud of witnesses', what is the greatest cost that you or I are likely to face for following Jesus? Rejection by friends who either think we're just not very cool or at worst may feel we have gone totally off our trolleys? Losing a job by sticking out on an issue of principle where something comes up that we feel is big enough to make a significant stand? Being called to missionary work in Africa where it is stiflingly hot; we have to learn the language, culture, customs; there is no television and very little money; and goodbye to all those promotion prospects?

None of these things really hold a candle to the sacrifices faced by some of our forebears. Could that be why they enjoyed a closer walk with God than we do? Could that be why heaven was more real to them? Could this be the reason for eternal realities impinging so visibly on their daily routines? Yes, I think so. But don't think this is just ancient church history. There are wonderful examples in recent times of exceptional Christians doing daring deeds. I want to look at a few of them next.

4

Modern Saints Who Point the Way

The pressure today against heaven being real can seem
overwhelming. But there are inspiring examples of modern saints who have believed in spite of overwhelming
opposition. And it seems to me that every time *any*
Christian takes a decision that is based on making eternal
values a priority, then that is one more victory for heaven,
one more miracle of God's unseen power at work.

The first time I remember feeling that victory was
when I heard about Jim Elliot. Jim was a missionary
to the Auca Indians in South America in the 1950s.
He was speared to death by the Indians and left floating
in a stream with some of his colleagues. I went to hear
his widow, Elizabeth, speak at a packed public hall in
Tunbridge Wells. She impressed me deeply by her calm
acceptance of his martyrdom. Her reaction showed her
heavenly perspective of what the life and death of her
husband really was all about. He had written in his diary:
'He is no fool who gives what he cannot keep to gain
what he cannot lose' (Elizabeth Elliot, *Shadow of the
Almighty*, Hodder and Stoughton, 1958).

Even so, when death on the mission field happened to
someone I knew, it came as a shock. At university I played
the guitar in a Christian band with Chris Begg. Chris had a

mass of fair hair, a dry sense of humour and a warm smile. He also had a good voice and was a dedicated Christian. When we had formed our band and rehearsed our songs, we felt God was leading us to go out and sing about Jesus to the young people of Tyneside. We had a few invitations from church youth groups, and things rolled from there. We weren't all that hot. But in the early sixties people were willing to listen to *anyone* who had a guitar in their hand, and so we sang our songs and gave our testimonies wherever we could.

Chris was especially good at reaching people in the rougher places we visited. Many times he would win kids over by his friendly interest in them. Chris seemed fearless. He would approach tough-looking kids on the street and share his faith with them in a way that I would never have dared. His total commitment to the cause of Christ was a rare thing in a young man of twenty-one.

We graduated. I started a career in accountancy and Chris started an evangelistic ministry with the organisation, Operation Mobilization. He married a lovely Swedish girl and joined an OM team working in India. Then on another milestone day I heard the news. Chris and his wife had been killed instantly when a truck had collided head-on with their car somewhere in India. I was devastated. Like Jim Elliot, a lifetime of service cut off in its prime. I could not make sense of it but one thing I knew. My friend Chris had crossed the line from time to eternity. He was now in heaven with Jesus. He had always lived with Christ as an everyday reality on earth and it seemed the most natural thing in the world that he should now be with him in heaven. Eternity seemed close, if full of mystery.

I spent some time in Uganda during the time of the regime of General Amin and the fear, brutality and violence of those days was appalling. The lawlessness in the capital, Kampala, was such that we constantly looked anxiously in the rear-view mirror of the car, since hold-ups at gunpoint after being tailed and rammed were not uncommon. At night we protected the doors to the house with huge sliding steel grills.

Archbishop Luwum of Kampala was one of the few men who stood up to General Amin. He fulfilled his calling as a church leader to stand up for righteousness and oppose oppression. When the specific persecution of Christians began (Amin was a Muslim) the Archbishop was interviewed on radio and asked what advice he had for Christians in Uganda. I think the interviewer expected that the wise thing would be to keep a low profile because otherwise there wouldn't be much of a church left in the country. But eternal goals dominated the bishop's agenda and he knew that he needed to keep his eyes on heaven rather than be cowed by problems on earth. His answer was very simple. 'We must be faithful,' he said. And he was. It led to Amin's anger – and the rest, sadly, is all too well known. Archbishop Janani Luwum was martyred – shot by Amin's police. It was a tragedy, but also a victory – an inspiring testimony to the power of eternal realities over the more immediate comforts of life that beckon us so strongly.

Sadly, Amin was not the only one to attack the church in Africa. A saintly African Christian who had lived through the Mau Mau reign of terror in Kenya surprised me in conversation one day. He told me of the vile oath of allegiance which many were forced to take during the 1950s. Many Christians refused to take any other oath than to follow Christ, protesting that they could pledge themselves to no other master. They faced torture and death. This old man remarked, 'Dying for Jesus was no problem to us – many faced it and many died. The difficult thing is living for Jesus – most of us find that far more difficult.'

Many African countries today face similar uncertainties. Does this cause Africa to be a cynical godless place, in which no Christian faith is found? Do you hear people constantly remark: 'I couldn't believe in your God because of what I have seen and been through?' No! The remarkable thing is that completely the reverse is the case. Revival situations abound. New churches spring up everywhere. There is a great awareness of God and a spiritual hunger. Heaven is real – perhaps because eternity is near. Can we say to a simple African Christian that he has nothing until he progresses to a civilised Western culture? Or would it be more appropriate to say that some of us should humbly admit that although we possess more possessions, we can still be paupers in the most significant and valuable areas of life? What life-changing possibilities might open up if heaven became more real to us!

What will change if heaven is real to us now?

Every time I attend a funeral or hear of someone's death, I pray that God will keep me from complacency and remind me always that I, too, am on a limited lease. Louis Armstrong sang 'We have all the time in the world', but we don't. As life goes by, time seems to go faster. When I was at school, the summer holidays seemed to go on forever. Nowadays a year goes by and I wonder where it went. Billy Graham, once interviewed on the *Larry King Live* show in America, was asked what had surprised him most about his life. His simple answer was: 'Its brevity.'

When as a child I slept and wept
   Time crept.
When as a youth, I laughed and talked
   Time walked.
When I became a full grown man
   Time ran.
And – older I 'daily' grew
   Time flew.
Soon I shall find – travelling on
   Time gone.

                             Anonymous

And what happens when our limited, brief 'time lease'
is up? Someone said to me recently, 'When I go, I hope
it's quick.' He added: 'If I could choose, I'd like to die in
my sleep, or next best would be a heart attack on the golf
course.' Many people are like that. They hope to avoid
prior knowledge of the end, and then to make it as swift as
possible. If you are diagnosed as having terminal cancer,
your relatives may keep this information from you. They
will think it is kinder that you don't know you are going
to die soon.

But is that really kind? Because the bottom line, of
course, is that *if we don't face death we don't get to
thinking about heaven*. Heaven only comes into the
picture if we honestly, thoughtfully face our mortality.

In fact, an old Church of England prayer asks that we
should be delivered from 'sudden death'. The reasoning
back then was that men and women *needed time* to prepare
for dying; to know that it's coming; to meditate on their
end; to thank God for their lives on earth; to commit
their souls to his divine love, mercy and forgiveness; and
to trustfully await what lies beyond. 'He who believes
in me shall live, even though he dies' (John 11:25)

Jesus assures us, adding, 'Today you will be with me in paradise' (Luke 23:43).

Having a certainty about life after death has a constant impact on your thinking. The length of your life becomes less important than experiencing the meaning of it. Of course, a life cut short is a cause of great grief to those left behind. Even the loss of an older person who has had far more than their three score years and ten may be grievous. But if the whole foundation of our thinking about existence has an eternal dimension with a loving God and a heaven for those who belong to him, the ultimate sting is withdrawn. The God who has always been there, who in fact gave us our life in the first place, moves us on to our eternal home and we need have no fear. We are part of the flow of eternity and that makes us secure.

So for a while forget the movies. Switch off your television. Lay aside the novels with supernatural themes. Let's explore something totally different which no one else can offer us. Infinitely better. Coming soon. Heaven, here we come.

Part Two

What Will Life Be Like in Heaven?

5

What Happens When I Die?

Dust to dust, spirit to spirit

I noticed an interesting thing when I was rereading the beginning of Genesis the other day. It tells us that 'The Lord God formed a man from the dust of the ground and breathed into his nostrils the breath of life, and the man became a living being' (Gen. 2:7). What struck me was that the raw material God started with was so very ordinary – dust of the ground. The next thing he did was quite extraordinary. He breathed into the body he had formed. He gave it the breath of life. The result was startling – the 'dust' ends up as a man.

The way life ends for you and me is just exactly this sequence of events in reverse. One minute a person is breathing and inhabiting a body. The body may be old and worn out. It may be malfunctioning due to disease or damaged by accident, but it is still living. A minute later everything is different. The person stops breathing, the brain stops sending its electrical pulses, the heart stops pumping blood. Something vital is missing – something which is much more than simply a cessation of mechanical activity. Whatever God breathed into the first body he created, has now departed. The breath of life is gone.

Immediately death comes, the degeneration of the body

commences. If you have ever lived in a hot country you know that funerals take place very soon after death. The human body – all those intricately made engineering and computer systems – is rapidly taking its next step: returning to the dust of the ground. The whole process of creation is reversed. But we don't despise the 'dust'. Throughout history the bodies of those who have died have been treated with reverence. The burial chambers in the pyramids of Egypt through to the tombstone memorials seen in today's cemeteries bear this out. We accord reverence to something which was once human, because human beings deserve dignity.

The book of Ecclesiastes has a neat summary of what is going on at this point. 'The dust returns to the ground it came from, and the spirit returns to God who gave it' (Eccles. 12:7). God made our bodies from the dust and so we return there. God gave us that thing which made us alive, our spirit, and that goes into eternity. Just as the Bible never attempts to prove that God exists, so it also assumes that everyone has a living spirit which goes on beyond death.

I have had people ask me: 'So *where* is a person's spirit located?' I can hear King David hooting with laughter as we put that question to him. Pen in hand, he will look up from writing Psalm 14 and say something like: 'You cannot be serious?' When we assure him some people would really like to know the answer, he puts his pen down and is lost in thought for a few moments. Then he looks up again and says: 'Here is a question for you. Where is any person's sense of humour located? How much does it weigh?' He is not laughing at us now, but looking dead serious.

'And what about being in love? Can you tell me how much that weighs? Or hatred – how many centimetres long is that?' This scene is becoming rather embarrassing so we politely thank this singer, songwriter and monarch, and bow out of his royal presence. He picks up his pen again with a chuckle as we leave.

I think he has made his point, hasn't he? We know that humour, love and hatred are real. But they are beyond scientific weighing and measuring. They are in a different realm. Science doesn't touch them because that is not its proper sphere. It is exactly the same with the spirit. The Bible takes it for granted that you have a living spirit which will return to God when you die. Genesis indicates that we are in totality a 'living being'.

Bertrand Russell spoke eloquently for the despair of many people when he stated his conviction that 'When I die, I rot.' Not so for St Paul: 'For me to live is Christ, and to die is gain' (Phil. 1:21). 'We eagerly await a Saviour from [heaven], the Lord Jesus Christ, who, by the power that enables him to bring everything under his control, will transform our lowly bodies so that they will be like his glorious body' (Phil. 3:20–21).

I once went to a funeral where at a certain point in the service the minister formally 'dismissed' the spirit from the body. I felt that was a very helpful thing. It reminded all of us there that the remains of the lovely saint of God whose funeral we were attending was not actually 'him'. The real 'him', his spirit, had left his body and had gone ahead. Now I don't happen to believe that the spirit actually departed at the moment of being dismissed. But the formality was a helpful picture of something that had already happened.

Sheldon Vanauken in his book, *A Severe Mercy* (Hodder, 1977), describes a feeling that the spirit of his much-loved wife Davy remained with him for some while after she died. He describes visiting places that had been special to them and sensing her 'presence' there. Eventually, however, as time goes by, the sense of her company fades and he seems to feel that she has departed and gone on ahead of him. This poses the question of whether these things are really true or simply subjective experiences. Does the spirit of a departed person stay around for a while or revisit or do they permanently depart to heaven?

In a tiny village on the west coast of Scotland, opposite the farmhouse where I was born, is a little grey stone church. On the hillside beside the church is the grave of my grandmother, Hester Sinclair. She was ninety-seven when she went to heaven. Sue and I frequently go to a cottage in the village for holidays and sometimes I go to 'visit granny'. I stand on the hillside by her little granite tombstone and thank God for her. She was one of the warm, happy influences of my childhood. I know she's not really there. It's just that it's very easy to conjure up her kindly face. It is purely an emotional subjective thing and in no way am I pretending actually to be in communication with her. Taken any further than this, I think, things can get out of hand.

I have known people try to continue a relationship with someone who has died because they cannot face life without them. While in the initial stages of bereavement that is perhaps entirely natural, the healthy attitude and the Christian one is surely to look back with gratitude, and to look forward to a new situation God has put us in with expectant hope and trust. To try and hold on to something that God has taken away is at best unhealthy and becomes quite wrong if we make any attempt to actually communicate with the spirit of someone who has died. Seances and the like are absolutely ruled out by Scripture.

But though our spirit returns to God who gave it, this is

not the end. We shall not be disembodied spirits for very long. We are promised a new body: one just like Christ's after his resurrection.

What will our new bodies be like?

How will this new body business work out? Do we get issued with a reconditioned version of the body we have on earth? Or is it completely different, a bit more like a ghost? The first Christians in churches all around the Mediterranean were debating the same issues.

Paul obviously thought a lot about heaven. There is a whole discussion on the subject in 1 Corinthians 15. He begins by saying that if Christ was raised from the dead, it is nonsense to suggest that we shall not also rise (1 Cor. 15:12). And logically, 'if Christ has not been raised, our preaching is useless and so is your faith' (1 Cor. 15:14). Paul calls a spade a spade. He goes on to conclude that, if all this is so, Christians really are a bunch of gullible idiots who deserve only pity – and a lot more pity than anyone else of whom he can think.

Paul then says emphatically, 'But Christ has indeed been raised from the dead, the first fruits of those who have fallen asleep' (1 Cor. 15:20). The resurrection has been described as one of the best attested facts in history. Therefore since Christ *did* rise from the dead, first it proves there is a resurrection. And second it shows the way that we are going to go if we die trusting in Christ.

Eugene Peterson in his New Testament paraphrase, *The Message*, has a way of drawing out meanings that we can relate to. This is how he expresses these verses, found in 1 Corinthians 15:35–52:

'What does this "resurrection body" look like?' If you

look at this question closely, you realise how absurd it is. There are no diagrams for this kind of thing. We do have a parallel experience in gardening. You plant a 'dead' seed; soon there is a flourishing plant. There is no visual likeness between seed and plant. You could never guess what a tomato would look like by looking at a tomato seed. What we plant in the soil and what grows out of it don't look anything alike. The dead body that we bury in the ground and the resurrection body that comes from it will be dramatically different.

You will notice that the variety of bodies is stunning. Just as there are different kinds of seeds, there are different kinds of bodies – humans, animals, birds, fish – each unprecedented in its form. You get a hint at the diversity of resurrection glory by looking at the diversity of bodies not only on earth but in the skies – sun, moon, stars – all these varieties of beauty and brightness. And we're only looking at the pre-resurrection 'seeds' – who can imagine what the resurrection 'plants' will be like!

This image of planting a dead seed and raising a live plant is a mere sketch at best, but perhaps it will help in approaching the mystery of the resurrection body – but only if you keep in mind that when we're raised, we're raised for good, alive forever! The corpse that's planted is no beauty, but when it's raised, it's glorious. Put in the ground weak, it comes up powerful. The seed sown is natural; the seed grown is supernatural – same seed, same body, but what a difference from when it goes down in physical mortality to when it is raised up in spiritual immortality!

We follow this sequence in Scripture: The First

What Happens When I Die?

Adam received life, the Last Adam is a life-giving Spirit. Physical life comes first, then spiritual – a firm base shaped from the earth, a final completion coming out of heaven. The First Man was made out of earth, and people since then are earthy; the Second Man was made out of heaven, and people now can be heavenly. In the same way that we've worked from our earthy origins, let's embrace our heavenly ends.

I need to emphasise, friends, that our natural, earthy lives don't in themselves lead us by their very nature into the kingdom of God. Their very 'nature' is to die, so how could they 'naturally' end up in the Life kingdom?

But let me tell you something wonderful, a mystery I'll probably never fully understand. We're not all going to die – but we are all going to be changed. You hear a blast to end all blasts from a trumpet, and in the time that you look up and blink your eyes – it's over. On signal from that trumpet from heaven, the dead will be up and out of their graves, beyond the reach of death, never to die again. At the same moment and in the same way, we'll all be changed.

I am no great gardener but I do enjoy the pleasurable sensation of planting seeds. Big ones are best; potatoes are very satisfying. It never ceases to amaze me that I can dig a little dark hole, stick a seed potato in it and cover it over. Then I can stand up and smile, confident that if I allow a little time to pass, great things will happen. I come back with my fork, stick it in and hey presto – a miracle! The body of the old seed has disappeared, or at best I may find a rotting shell which is hardly recognisable; but instead there are several new bodies, rather like the old one I planted but actually much fresher, firmer and nicer.

So the present body you and I move around is the 'seed' of the resurrection body. We may have questions about how the dead can be raised when there is probably nothing left of the many billions of people who have died over the centuries. And if we try to simplify the picture in our minds by envisaging God recreating bones and flesh peacefully laid to rest in a coffin years ago, it really isn't as simple as that; what about those whose bodies have been irreparably maimed in fatal road accidents or completely destroyed by a terrorist bomb blast? Much more common to our experience, what about those who have been cremated? Does God somehow gather up what remains thereof and construct a new body?

Paul basically tells us not to be so arrogant as to think we will always be able to work out how God will do things. What *will* be significant is that our spirits will be housed in a new body which God has designed to ensure it is entirely suitable for our new environment. You will be utterly comfortable with yourself, your surroundings, your friends and your God.

The new body will be alive forever – that's quite an improvement on the old model which wears out around three score years and ten. But in heaven you and I will still be the same people deep inside. That's because whatever it is that is the essential me and you is our spirit. Paul spells out our uniqueness as he names that part of us which God can communicate with to reassure us that we belong to him. 'The Spirit himself testifies with our spirit that we are God's children' (Rom. 8:16).

We certainly can have sufficient confidence to look forward to many good things. Our fears that we might move on to a new life that would be some kind of ethereal cloud-hopping, harp-playing spirit life can go out of the window. The best that we have enjoyed here will continue, but without those things that taint this life.

David Winter expresses it well:

> The 'resurrection' life is a life of power, achievement, splendour, beauty. It has everything good from this earthly life, but without the things that make it earth-bound, limited and frustrating. Over everything on earth hangs the dark shadow of time. We never seem to have enough of it to do the things we should like to do, to become the people we ought to be or to get to know others as we should like to know them. (*Hereafter*, p. 73)

I am really looking forward to my new resurrection body! Ever since the car accident which left my right side partially paralysed, I've been looking forward to the day when I shall be able to enjoy a lot of things I have really missed over the past few years. I shall be able to put my walking boots on and hike for miles over the hills. I shall be able to run and play tennis again. (If everything is perfect, perhaps every serve will be an ace.) I shall ski again, hurtling down the heavenly pistes with incredible style and performing perfect parallel turns which I couldn't even do in my prime on earth. I shall carry little children on my shoulders and take them on tours round the heavenly gardens (right now any child travelling on my shoulders would do so at its peril since one of my regular falls would quite likely cause him to take a tumble). I will windsurf at incredible speed across heavenly bays with sun-blessed beaches and will be so athletic that I shall never fall off my board. What a wonderful thing to have a new body!

Many of us may have struggled with bodies we didn't really like. Or perhaps we feel that other people don't like us the way we are now. So if you ever felt too tall or too short – don't worry. If you had a bit of a complex about being too fat or too thin – you won't have a problem there. If you were self-conscious about your nose, ears or feet – it won't happen again. If you worried about being a slightly clumsy person, or not very sporty or whatever, don't worry about the future.

We shall have perfect bodies. Glorious bodies. Transformed and redeemed bodies. They will be just like Jesus's resurrection body and you will be utterly happy with yours and so will everyone else. After his resurrection, Jesus certainly didn't waft round the place and no one saw him sitting on a cloud playing a harp. He walked along a road talking with friends. He told people where to catch the best fish. He cooked a barbecue breakfast on a beach. He even ate some fish. This was certainly no ghostly spirit floating around. He had a real body you could reach out and touch – exactly as he invited Thomas with all his doubts to do.

A new mind

One of the legacies of my car accident is a hidden disability. Because of the damage to my nervous system and the medication I have been on since the accident, my powers of concentration (which I can't claim were ever very great) are somewhat limited and try as it may, my mind goes cross-eyed after an hour or two of intense concentration. The batteries just seem to give up and need recharging.

But what about this – I am going to get a new mind in heaven! Of course, I am fervently hoping there are no physics exams in heaven, because even if my new mind could romp through the questions (and I'm sure it would) just thinking about physics exams makes me feel funny and I have a nasty notion this is so deep-seated that it might stay with me.

Actually, our minds will not be cluttered with any bad memories, depressing thoughts or sadness. We shall not carry over any of the baggage which clouded our minds on earth. Way back in Old Testament times Isaiah was quite clear about this: 'I will create new heavens and a new earth. The former things will not be remembered, nor will they come to mind' (Isa. 65:17). At first sight this could look like a bit of a puzzle because our personalities include the memories and experiences we have. However, I think it's pretty clear that 'the former things' cannot refer to *everything* we have left behind in a former life. (Otherwise how could we recognise our friends and family, or even know deep in our spirits that we are the same person we were on earth?) No, I don't think everything is obliterated, but it is the 'old order of things' which Revelation 21:4 explains is all that pain, sorrow and hurt. None of that will be remembered.

Then there is another significant aspect to having a new mind which Paul describes like this: 'Now we see but a poor reflection as in a mirror; then we shall see face to face. Now I know in part; then I shall know fully, even as I am fully known' (1 Cor. 13.12). On earth, there are limits to how far we can go, what our minds can grasp. But one day we shall know fully.

My eldest daughter Naomi currently works with adults who have learning difficulties. She teaches them basic skills like how to go shopping, how to use leisure without watching TV all the time, how to cook a meal or get on a train. They are mostly happy individuals, but aware of their limitations. In one sense you could say there is nothing wrong with their simple enjoyment of life, but what a wonderful thing it will be for those who have endured these limitations through their lives but who trust Jesus, to arrive in heaven and enjoy the enhanced faculty of a new mind.

If you have ever suffered a nervous breakdown or mental illness there is comfort for those of us like that too. I have experienced a share of physical pain here on earth, but I really think the anguish of a tortured mind is far, far harder to bear. To live with the sense that you are losing your mind, to constantly battle with depressive thoughts or haunting memories is terrible, but one day we shall have total release. Our new minds will be as clear and healthy as a bubbling mountain stream. They will be as calm and peaceful as an old English millpond.

So, with our glorious new bodies and new minds, what can we know about the new home we are destined for?

6

A Picture of Heaven

There are 621 references to heaven or the heavens in the Bible. First and foremost it is the dwelling place of God, and of those closely associated with him. In the Old Testament the Hebrew word *samayim* and in the New Testament the Greek *ouranos* are used. Just as in English, 'heaven' seems to be interchangeable with 'the heavens'.

God's sovereign rule

King Solomon, surrounded by unparalleled wealth, power and culture, had a simple wish. He wanted to construct a building which would give people a sense of God's presence. In spite of his immense resources as the richest man in the world, he makes a humble confession: 'The heavens, even the highest heaven, cannot contain you. How much less this temple I have built.' And yet this omnipotent God has compassion on us, and actively cares for us. Solomon prays elsewhere: 'Hear from heaven, your dwelling place, and when you hear, forgive' (1 Kgs. 8:30).

The Psalms express this same confidence in the God of heaven: 'I will lift up my eyes to you, to you whose throne is in heaven' (Ps. 123:1). God's reign in heaven spills out to earth and at times can be clearly seen. When King Nebuchadnezzar got a bit above himself and began meditating on how great, mighty and majestic he was, God decided he needed a little humbling. Nebuchadnezzar lived like an animal for a period of time. He describes in his own words how he recovered: 'I raised my eyes towards heaven and my sanity was restored.' He goes on to praise 'the Most High; I honour and glorify him who lives for ever.' Nebuchadnezzar's appreciation of God who reigns in heaven has certainly changed: 'His dominion is an eternal dominion; his kingdom endures from generation to generation . . . he does as he pleases with the powers of heaven and the people of the earth' (Dan. 5:28–35).

The Bible talks again and again about heaven being the place where God is at home and earth being where we live. Isaiah sums it up: 'Heaven is my throne and the earth is my footstool' (Isa. 66:1).

God's glory prophesied

Ezekiel describes his vision of the scene in heaven as the voice of Almighty God is heard:

> Then there came a voice from above the expanse over their heads as they stood with lowered wings. Above the expanse over their heads was what looked like a throne of sapphire, and high above on the throne was a figure like that of a man. I saw that from what appeared to be his waist up he looked like glowing metal, as if full of fire, and that from there down he looked like fire; and brilliant light surrounded him. Like the appearance of a rainbow in the clouds on a rainy day, so was the radiance around him. This

was the appearance of the likeness of the glory of the Lord. (Ezek.1:25–28)

As expected, Ezekiel uses several 'likes': 'like a throne', 'like a man', 'like glowing metal', 'like fire', 'like a rainbow', and the whole thing is 'the likeness of the glory of the Lord'. If nothing in the Bible is there by accident, then we have to believe that there is some significance in all this, however odd it may appear at first glance. Thrones, precious jewels, glowing metal, fire, rainbows, brilliant lights . . . the prophet was using language to describe things we know on this earth to be precious, radiant and dazzling.

Some of the images that are used in the Bible don't always appeal to us. But the prophets who saw the visions were literally lost for words, and having to use earthly language, which was completely inadequate. I personally feel quite glad of that! Heaven is so wonderful that no words on earth can ever come anywhere near to communicating how amazing it is.

Where Jesus dwells

Heaven has also been the abode of Jesus since – well, since all eternity. The very first verse of the Bible starts: 'In the beginning God . . .' Jesus was there with God the Father and the Holy Spirit involved in the creation process, as the Hebrew noun *elohim* (translated God) shows. This word is plural, and commentators have called it 'the plural of majesty'.

John's Gospel emphasises this: 'In the beginning was the Word, and the Word was with God, and the Word was God. He was with God in the beginning' (John 1:1). Luke describes the scene when Jesus leaves the earth: 'He was taken up before their very eyes, and a cloud hid him from their sight' (Acts 1:9). The angels who then appeared told the disciples quite directly where Jesus had gone. 'This same Jesus who has been taken from you into heaven, will come back . . .'

Heaven is Jesus's home. He came from there, and returned there.

Where the Holy Spirit dwells

On that memorable day when a confused bunch of disheartened disciples was transformed into a powerful fighting force, Luke records: 'Suddenly a sound like the blowing of a violent wind came from heaven and filled the whole house. They saw what seemed to be tongues of fire that separated and came to rest on each of them' (Acts 2:2, 3). On the day the Church was born in Jerusalem, the Holy Spirit came from heaven to fill those first disciples, in just the way Jesus had promised.

'When the Counsellor comes, whom I will send to you from the Father . . . you also must testify for you have been with me from the beginning' (John 15: 26, 27). And testify they certainly did, enabled by the power of the Holy Spirit. Jesus had promised it to them: 'You will receive power when the Holy Spirit comes on you; and you will be my witnesses' (Acts 1:8).

So the initial power boost that the early Church received as it lifted off the launch pad, and the daily power every Christian today needs to live like Jesus come from the Holy Spirit – direct from heaven.

Understood from the start

Old Testament hope

The Old Testament is shot through with the idea that the spirits of those who die go to a place described by the Hebrew word *Sheol*. No judgment of the righteous or the unrighteous is implied there. It is a waiting place for all departed souls. There is more than a hint however, of what the departed are waiting for: judgment and justice. Psalm 49 gives a clear picture of the fate of those who 'trust in themselves' – they will 'decay in the grave' (verse 14).

On the other hand, there are those who have put their faith in the Lord. David sings, 'You have made known to me the path of life' (Ps. 16:11) and looks beyond death to a time when 'God will redeem my life from the grave; he will surely take me to himself' (Ps. 49:15).

'You will fill me with joy in your presence, with eternal pleasures at your right hand' (Ps. 16:11). Our ultimate joy and happiness is being in God's immediate company. This is the kind of pleasure that lasts not for a moment, or for a dream holiday, or even a happy lifetime. This pleasure is 'eternal'. It's almost a return to the Garden of Eden, a place of wonder and bliss, where we feel at home, in the presence of God.

So throughout the Old Testament God's plan of salvation unfolds. From the call to Abraham and the promise of founding a great nation with him, the Old Testament traces the history of the Israelites, and the promise of a coming Messiah who will save his people and inaugurate a new, peaceful kingdom based on righteousness and justice.

New Testament hope

The New Testament opens with the Lord Jesus Christ coming to earth. He deals with the awfulness of sin by dying in our place. He provides us with power through his Spirit to live in every heart that welcomes him. He also promises an entirely new thing: freedom from the presence of evil, and a life forever with God in a place that he would provide. That is to say, a home in heaven!

> In my Father's house are many rooms; if it were not so, I would have told you. I am going there to prepare a place for you. And if I go and prepare a place for you, I will come back and take you to be with me that you also may be where I am. (John 14: 2, 3)

As I struggle to find a way to visualise what my life will be like in heaven, pictures of something fairly concrete are very helpful. Those times when I have sat on a hillside, gazing at a sunset and soaking up the beauty. Inhaling the intoxicating scent of a bright red rose in our garden on a sunny day and exhaling a silent thank you to God for the exquisite delicacy of his creation. Squeezing my wife's hand in warm communication, rejoicing in God's love for us and our love for one another. The experiences of all the best moments of this life seem to me to be a tangible echo of what heaven will be like.

Another little snippet of Jesus's teaching, which I think is highly significant, comes when some of his disciples are quizzing him about rewards. Having heard some hard words about rich men finding it tough to enter the kingdom of heaven (an extraordinary idea to Jewish people where prosperity was said to indicate God's blessing) the disciples are feeling blown away. They reckon no one stands a chance of being saved. Jesus encourages them with a picture of wonderful rewards for those who have been faithful to him and says that everything will be sorted out 'at the renewal of all things, when the Son of Man sits on his glorious throne' (Matt. 19:28). He could have used any words he liked. But he didn't talk about the end of the world and the destruction of everything, but rather 'the renewal of all things'.

Jesus also talked quite a lot about his return to the earth: what we call the *parousia*, or Second Coming. Jesus promises: 'At that time the sign of the Son of Man will appear in the sky . . . they will see the Son of Man coming on the clouds of the sky with power and great glory' (Matt. 24:30). And when the disciples stood squinting up into the sky on the day that Jesus ascended, two angels suddenly appeared with some good news. 'This same Jesus, who has been taken from you into heaven, will come back in the same way you have seen him go into heaven' (Acts 1:11). The angels confirm it. He is coming back to planet earth.

So if you trust in Jesus don't let anyone ever tell you that your spirit won't live forever, that the real you deep inside won't go on into eternity with your God.

Paul talks about those who 'sleep in the Lord' and about his desire to 'depart and be with the Lord'. Both of these are pictured in enthusiastic terms: 'For me to live is Christ, to die is gain' (Phil. 1:21).

Dying was certainly 'gain' for Lazarus, in the story told by Jesus. He was a diseased beggar at the gate of the rich Dives. Lazarus had a bad deal in this life, but when the time came for both him and Dives to die, Jesus portrays them in different territories of the spirit world, with 'a great chasm' fixed between them. The righteous poor man is pictured as already in the comforting presence of other righteous people. The rich man is in a place of suffering, because he had lived a selfish and unrepentant life (Luke 16:19–31).

Where did Jesus go when he died?

At boarding-school I can remember being very confused by the creed we said in the service every Sunday. I can remember thinking what a strange thing it was to say that we believe Jesus 'descended into hell'. (The New Testament uses the Greek word *Hades* which means exactly the same as *Sheol*.) It caused a jarring sensation every week because I knew very well that this would be the last place Jesus would want to go. Being a critical know-all, I put the phrase down to the school chaplain not knowing any better and getting the service wrong each week.

Later, of course, I discovered that earlier versions of the Bible and prayer book translated *Hades* as 'hell'. We think of the whole realm where Satan and his demons have their home as being hell. That is certainly different from the waiting place of departed spirits, Sheol.

Jesus descended into a place of departed spirits. Even as He died on the cross, He reassured the repentant thief: 'I tell you the truth, today you will be with me in Paradise' (Luke 23:43). The literal meaning of Paradise is 'a garden'. One thing that seems clear from this is that after the grave, there is a wonderful place where the righteous departed spirits wait in an eager happy state with Jesus. Even if this is not the final destination, Jesus obviously wanted you and me to know that there is a place of beauty and peace. Whatever it is like, you will enjoy being there.

What was Jesus's resurrection body like?

Jesus's post-resurrection appearances reveal some intriguing bits of information. The first thing I noticed was that Jesus's facial appearance must have changed. Even those closest to him did not recognise him.

The first was Mary Magdalene. Meeting Jesus in the garden by the tomb, Mary was grief-stricken. She didn't recognise him and thought he must be the gardener. Neither Jesus's voice or his appearance gave him away. It was only when Jesus said her name that she suddenly lit up in recognition. He must have had a particular affectionate way of saying it that she recognised. But it was only when he deliberately gave himself away. Obviously his appearance and his voice were not readily recognisable.

Then there were the two disciples who walked seven miles along the footpath to Emmaus from Jerusalem. When a stranger joined them, they were flabbergasted to find that he apparently knew nothing of recent events in Jerusalem. But then he talked to them of the Scriptures, of how the events they were talking about fulfilled all the Old Testament forecasts of God's plans for the future, and the two disciples were deeply moved. They urged the stranger to stay with them at Emmaus and, as dusk turned to darkness, they all sat down to dinner. The stranger said grace – and suddenly their 'eyes were opened and they recognised him' (Luke 24:31).

Was it some mannerism in the particular way Jesus said grace? Was it some form of words he used as he asked a blessing on the meal? Or was it some supernatural lifting of a veil which had been placed over their eyes? We don't know for sure.

The Gospel of John gives us a third cameo in chapter 21. In the days following the execution of Jesus, his disciples struggled. They had expected a new kingdom to arrive, and it hadn't. Finally Simon Peter returned to the sea to fish, and the others joined him. They caught nothing, all night. They were depressed when they stepped into the boat, but by five o'clock in the morning their tempers must have been frayed as well. Then along came a stranger, who called to them.

'Haven't you any fish?' I think it is quite likely that the disciples muttered that if they *had* got a nice sloshy wet fish and been closer into the shore, they would happily hurl it at the stranger. A couple of the more polite disciples probably shouted back, 'No'.

'Throw your net on the right side of the boat and you will find some fish.'

I bet that didn't improve tempers in the boat! It was Peter – rash, impulsive – who said: 'Let's give it one more try.' And of course the net was so full of fish it nearly sank the boat. It wasn't the voice. It wasn't the face – he was too far away. It was the miraculous catch that did it. Peter leapt overboard and struck out for the shore. The others followed in the boat, the weight of fish tearing the net. When they landed they saw a fire, barbecuing fish, and some bread. The atmosphere was somewhat strained, but the stranger simply said, 'Bring some of the fish you have caught.' The disciples dragged the net on shore and counted the catch. One hundred and fifty-three fish. The best catch in years. The man barbecuing fish simply said, 'Come and have breakfast.'

Now here is the curious thing. I would have expected these closest friends of Jesus who had followed him round for three years to have bounded up to him with a warm greeting, to give him a bear hug or at the very least a hearty handshake and a 'good to see you again!' But there is none of that. All that John's Gospel tells us is that none of the disciples dared ask him 'Who are you?' They knew it was the Lord, and they were dumbstruck. So Jesus brought the bread and fish and handed it around. Why didn't they greet Jesus? Why didn't they dare say anything? They obviously knew who it was, but they could see that while it was the same person, he was different. His resurrection body was different from his previous body. Some things had changed, but it was the same person.

I don't think we shall ever understand this, but we can see that he was ordinary enough to stand on a beach, shout across the water, light a fire and prepare a meal. He had the same supernatural knowledge that could lead to miracles – directing them to where he knew the fish were. But on the evening of the first Easter Sunday, when the disciples were holed up in a house with all the doors locked, Jesus had no problem getting through their security and entered the room through a locked door (John 20:19). His resurrection body was obviously different and could pass through solid objects. But it still bore the scars of his ordeal. He even identified himself positively to the disciples by showing them the scars on his hands and side.

Thomas, of course, was the one who had most difficulty believing Christ had risen. In an uncharacteristic move, Jesus gave evidence to someone who had said they would not believe without evidence. Again entering through locked doors, Jesus held out his hands to him and said, 'Put your finger here; see my hands' (John 20:27). Thomas had vehemently said he couldn't believe unless he saw the nail marks in the hands and put his finger where the nails were. All this tells us that, though Jesus could appear and disappear at will, pass through solid objects and disguise his appearance, his body was none the less real, in some special way. You could see it. You could touch it. You could put your finger into the nail holes, and feel the flesh and bones.

In the account in Luke's Gospel, Jesus suddenly 'stood among them' and knowing how this would startle any normal human, he greeted them in the traditional way, now given a new significance: 'Peace be with you' (Luke 24:36). They didn't just get a fright; they thought they were seeing a ghost. Jesus is his usual reassuring self. 'Why are you troubled, and why do doubts rise in your minds? Look at my hands and my feet. It is I myself! Touch me and see; a ghost does not have flesh and bones, as you see I have' (Luke 24:38, 39). Without further ado he pulled back his sleeves and held out his hands for inspection. Then he reached down and pulled his flowing clothes up from his feet – they too were terribly scarred from his crucifixion.

If you were a disciple, do you think you would have been convinced and enlightened by now? Well, these chaps weren't! 'They still did not believe it because of joy and amazement' (Luke 24:41). I suppose if we had been there we would have been so bowled over by the surprise of it all, we could just not have taken it all in. Have you found Jesus very patient with you? He certainly was there with that bunch.

'Do you have anything here to eat?' he asked. I am sure that he was not actually hungry, but wanted to show them he was the same person with a similar though different body. They gave him a piece of boiled fish and he took it and ate it while they gawped at him. That seemed to do the trick. Ghosts can't eat fish. They were convinced about his resurrection body. Having got that settled, Jesus got down to important business. 'He opened their minds so they could understand the Scriptures' (Luke 24:45). This was no ordinary Bible study even for Jesus. It was his last on earth. He left final instructions, and told the disciples to stay in Jerusalem 'until you have been clothed with power from on high' (Luke 24:49).

Jesus led them out of the house and down the road to a spot near the village of Bethany. It was a couple of miles south-east of Jerusalem and they followed the path down the Kidron Valley out of the city and up the other side on to the Mount of Olives. He stopped near the village and as he lifted his hands to bless the disciples something happened. While he was blessing them, his resurrected body seemed gently to float away from them. A cloud soon hid him from view and he was gone.

The disciples accepted that he had gone back to heaven, and didn't waste time looking for him. They got straight down to the new job they'd been given. I'm guessing, but I reckon that as they waited for the Holy Spirit to come to them, they talked over all they had learned about the new resurrection body. As their confident new lifestyle indicates, they firmly expected to see Jesus again. They must have known that the normal processes of illness and old age could no longer touch Jesus. They would meet again as the same person they had come to know, admire and love. I don't think the mystery of how this would happen bothered them, and it shouldn't bother us. They had enough certainties to go on, and so do we.

7

Angels

Heaven and angels go together in the minds of many people. When I saw my first angel it wasn't a real one, just a picture. The only Sunday school I ever attended was in a little village called Burwash in Sussex. The sleepy village was a picturesque place, famous as the home of Rudyard Kipling. There were only a handful of us children, but we had an excellent teacher and I have happy memories of that Sunday school – and of my first angel. It was huge. You came in past the battered blue door of the Sunday-school hall and there it was – straight ahead of you. It was a classic 'old masters' type of painting, depicting activities in a corner of heaven. There were a number of apostles standing round, the odd lion or two lying down with lambs, and then this angel, who rather dominated proceedings.

He was in mid-flight, with arms and legs bent as if running furiously. Obviously he was on an errand and going there fast. His face was kindly but firmly set beneath curly blond hair. But what struck me most were the wings. Vast, classic, shining, gold wings! Whenever I walked into the room I always glanced up at him to check those gold wings were still shining. During lessons I would sometimes try and guess as to where he might be going. His slightly forbidding expression made quite an impression on me. He seemed to be saying: 'I hope you are behaving yourself down there!'

This was my early introduction to angels. I knew that they were in the Bible and having seen this picture of a 'real one' at six years old, I had no doubt that they were real, and looked exactly like the slightly disapproving fellow in my picture. As an adult, I accepted angels must be real, though I had little conviction as to the details. Who they were, what they did and where they operated were a mystery to me. Over the years, however, people I trusted told me of their experiences of angels. Turning back to the Bible I discovered that there is a fair amount we are told, and quite a few things we can deduce.

Who are they?

Created, not divine, as servants of God   Angels have greater powers than we do, but like us, are subject to God's authority. They must have to keep checking in with 'headquarters' to find out what God has been planning for them as their next project.

Many, many of them   At the time of Jesus's arrest, Peter whipped out his sword and took a swipe at the high priest's servant, chopping off his ear. Jesus assured Peter that there was no need to defend him. 'Do you think I cannot call on my Father, and he will at once put at my disposal more than twelve legions of angels?' (Matt. 26:53). A Roman legion had six thousand soldiers. Twelve legions equals 72,000. Jesus said there were more than that available to swoop in and rescue him if he wished at the snap of his fingers.

The total number of angels is vast. The Bible mentions

one hundred million (Rev. 5:11), but even that doesn't tell us that this is the whole headcount!

The Bible also describes different types of angel.

Seraphs　　If the number of wings angels possess is any kind of indication of status, seraphs do pretty well. They have six wings, though they only use two for flying (Isa. 6:2). John describes what sounds like four seraphs he saw, each with six wings; though he refers to them as 'living creatures' rather than labelling them as angels (Rev. 4:8). But they were certainly doing what angels do all the time because he tells us they never stop saying 'Holy, holy, holy, is the Lord God Almighty who was, and is, and is to come.' The seraph referred to in Isaiah's vision (Isa. 6:6) cleansed his lips from guilt by using a red hot coal.

Cherubs　　have only four wings, but when Ezekiel saw them, 'the glory of the God of Israel was above them' (Ezek. 10:19–21). Hebrews tells us that cherubs had an important job to do while Israel was wandering around the wilderness with the Ark. Above the Ark there were 'cherubim of the Glory' (Heb. 9:5). It seems as though they functioned as if they were police motorbike outriders accompanying the limousine of a monarch; guarding, guiding and attending, they made sure all was well.

Some angels are described as 'mighty angels' (Rev. 5:2; 10:1). Whether this means we shall meet some extra strong angels in heaven, I'm not sure. Certainly the one who is described as having mighty vocal chords sounds as if he would fit that description since he was 'proclaiming in a loud voice, "Who is worthy to break the seals and open the scroll?"' Power and might pour from the descriptions in Revelation. Another mighty angel was clothed in a cloud, with a rainbow above his head. His legs are described as being as powerful as 'fiery pillars'.

Archangels are in a class of their own. I may have to apologise if I am offending any of you angels watching me write this, but it does suggest to me that there is a kind of chain of command amongst angels – and therefore throughout the whole organisation of heaven. If God has set people in authority on this earth and given them responsibilities, then why not in heaven? Archangels certainly have an important place and significant task. In fact if you and I are around when Jesus comes back, the first we shall know about it will be an ear-splitting archangel shout accompanied by a blast from the trumpet section of God's mighty orchestra (1 Thess. 4:16).

I am looking forward to finding out whether there are several archangels or only one. The archangel Michael truly had a demanding job to do '. . . when he was disputing with the devil' (Jude 9). He is also pictured as one of the leaders of heaven's armies at a time when there was a war in heaven. And Michael has been some fighter for a very long time. Daniel describes how he wins a 21-day battle against a demon who was exercising influence over the Persian Empire (Dan. 10:13). 'Michael and his angels fought against the dragon, and the dragon and his angels fought back' (Rev. 12:7). Michael is also described as 'the great prince who protects [the people of God]' (Dan. 12:1).

The Church of England has two archbishops: York and Canterbury. So maybe there is more than one archangel or perhaps Michael reigns supreme. If you are an Anglican by conviction you probably will assume there must be more than one, since heaven must be modelled on the

Church of England. And then on second thoughts maybe you won't!

The other angel whose name you need to remember is Gabriel. God chose him to tell Zechariah the good news that at last his wife was going to have a baby. The baby was going to be John the Baptist, who would be the cause of numerous parties in heaven, as he would 'bring back to the Lord their God' many people (Luke 1:16). As Gabriel stood in the holiest place of the temple, to the right of the altar with incense rising on it, poor old Zechariah was terrified out of his wits. Seeing angels in heaven will probably be awesome, but to be actually standing in front of one a few feet away, on earth, we have good reason to be bowled over. Zechariah calmed down when the angel told him not to be afraid. Then he got all worked up again when Gabriel told him how very important he was in the heavenly hierarchy: 'I am Gabriel. I stand in the presence of God, and I have been sent to speak to you' (Luke 1:19). Gabriel then had a further and rather unpleasant message to tell Zechariah. He had to point out just how much he had blundered by not believing what God said. I am sure Zechariah was about to apologise, but he found that the second promise Gabriel had made (that God would make him dumb until the baby was born) had actually come true immediately. No faith was required for that one.

Heavenly work

I was quite surprised at how many different times in the Bible the activities of angels are mentioned. They seem to get around all over the place. I found it helpful to separate their activities in heaven from those on earth. The major activity of heaven is worship, in which angels are certainly very involved. 'All the angels were standing around the throne . . . they fell down on their faces before the throne and worshipped God' (Rev. 7:11).

We have some wonderfully varied talent in our church, and worship on a Sunday morning includes keyboard players, guitar players, drummers, a double bass, flute and violin. I love it. We sing modern worship songs and what my father-in-law calls 'real hymns' as well. I have the privilege of travelling round many churches and on about half of my Sundays I am worshipping with some other fellowship and enjoying coming before God's throne in the particular style which their members lead.

Quite *how* the angels worship is something we can only speculate about. Maybe they sing the latest Graham Kendrick songs, hot from Spring Harvest. Perhaps, because they must be very old, they find these newfangled worship songs a bit much, and stick with singing Wesley's hymns. We can only guess at what goes on. But what we can be sure of is that our best moments of worship here on earth can only ever be a tiny taste of the wonder we shall one day share with the angels as they worship round the throne.

Angels also have important things to do as God's servants. In this they seem to have an affinity with us. One of them is quick to point this out to John when, in his vision in Revelation, he is about to fall down and worship a dazzling angel. The angel stops him with a heartwarming description of his relationship with John: 'I am a fellow-servant with you and with your brothers and sisters who hold to the testimony of Jesus' (Rev. 19:10).

I suppose I tend to think that rich people who have servants are pampered. When we think of God and his servants the angels, we have to think very differently. God has servants because there are important things to be done and he deserves to be served with dedication. That is exactly what the angels feel as they go to it with vim and vigour every day in the eternity of heaven. If you were looking forward to an angel as some kind of personal Jeeves, looking after your every need, then think again. You will be joining the angels as a fellow servant.

As you take a tour round the courts of heaven you will discover another angelic activity. They have really inquisitive minds. They like to study things. When Peter was writing to a bunch of Christians who had been in Jerusalem on the day of Pentecost, he mentioned the 'new birth into a living hope' which the Christians had experienced (1 Pet. 1:3). He recalled how the prophets of the Old Testament would love to have known more about the time when Christ would come. After their time, says Peter, the Holy Spirit revealed the precise details of how salvation would be achieved, and the early, clouded promises became known to Christians. Then Peter makes the most extraordinary statement: 'Even angels long to look into these things' (1 Pet. 1:12). So angels have an intense desire to look into the mystery of grace, salvation and revelation. The immense ache they have to be involved in this comes out in the Greek translation which means 'to stoop and look intently'.

Angels seem also to be affected by people's actions here on earth. When Paul wrote to the proud and self-satisfied Corinthian church, he wanted to stress that being an apostle was a tough life. Paul says that he is foolish and dishonoured for Christ, that he has known hunger, homelessness, overwork, verbal abuse, brutal persecution and slander. He is regarded as the dregs, the garbage of the earth. He caps all this with the most extraordinary statement: 'It seems to me that God has put us apostles on display . . . like those condemned to die in the arena. We have been made a spectacle to the whole universe, to angels as well as to human beings' (1 Cor. 4:9). A spectacle to angels. What an extraordinary concept.

Then the Gospel of Luke tells us: 'In the same way, I tell you, there is rejoicing in the presence of the angels of God over one sinner who repents' (Luke 15:10). So angels, like us, celebrate an event which causes great joy and relief. Just a few days ago my son Ben heard that he had been accepted for medical school. Ben had worked hard towards this goal for nearly four years. When he finally got a place our whole family went bananas and then collapsed with relief. The angels share this feeling! They look down and see the good things God is doing and the changes in people's lives, and then they call their friends and have a party.

Angels also delight in acting as guides in heaven and explaining any puzzling things to new arrivals. When John is transported to heaven and sees quite a few things that he doesn't understand, an angel comes alongside to help and says, 'Why are you astonished? I will explain to you the mystery.' (Rev. 17:7).

I have always had immense feelings of satisfaction explaining things to people. I spent many happy hours when our children were small reaching for my potted book of English history on our sitting-room bookshelf and turning the pages seeking the answer to some puzzle. With a child snuggled under my arm I happily explained the delights of King Arthur burning the cakes, or the terrors of ragged Scots defeated at Culloden. It's a great feeling to explain a puzzle to someone and see a look of recognition and satisfaction come over their face. Angels enjoy that too.

There must be a lot of puzzles about heaven and plenty

of mysteries for the angels to enjoy explaining. There will be all the delight of God's redeemed creation in a new heaven and new earth where perhaps we shall find plants, animals and all kinds of wonders which expert angels will conduct us through. They will make fascinating guides because they have lived and worked in heaven for an awfully long time.

It seems angels are also good administrators. Paul in Ephesians says that God has placed Jesus 'far above all rule and authority, power and dominion, and every title that can be given, not only in the present age but also in the one to come' (Eph. 1:21). The decisions that God makes must be handed down the hierarchy of authority and God's will is to be carried out by those given power and responsibility under him. Angels must surely be included in this administrative structure. An awesome responsibility delegated to angels will be to assist God at the end of time in the process of judgment.

What a wonderful time that will be, when we are free to love God and do good and join the angels in worship. There will be no one around to tempt us, deceive us or spoil anything. What a wonderful new world! As you can see, the angels are heavily involved in running operations in heavenly places now. But they have an executive function which brings them from heaven to earth for all sorts of activities that are very helpful to us. Let's take a look at some.

Earthly work

In the Old Testament there are numerous occasions when God allowed his chosen people to be disciplined by the action of another nation. Angels wait to put into effect his decisions and I think they must be constantly surprised by how few times God sends them in acts of judgment to earth. God seems to be remarkably patient in putting up with the world's disobedience and evil. There are many times as I read the newspapers, see the TV news and hear about people's lives around me that I marvel God does not send an angel to fall in judgment.

But angels *are* sometimes sent to carry out judgment on earth. Sennacherib coming to threaten Jerusalem was a classic Old Testament example. The King of Syria had sent messages 'against the Lord God and against his servant Hezekiah' (2 Chr. 32:16, 17). As King Hezekiah and the prophet Isaiah 'cried out in prayer to heaven about this', God 'sent an angel who annihilated all the fighting men and leaders and officers in the camp of the Assyrian king' (2 Chr. 32:21). The angels acted decisively under God's orders in judgment.

Ministering spirits

The supreme struggle of Jesus was in the Garden of Gethsemane. There is still a grove of olive trees where the original garden was. I sat there once under their shade and visualised Jesus on his knees with his head fervently bowed under a gnarled olive. 'Being in anguish, he prayed more earnestly.' It was a time of immense need and God sent help. 'An angel from heaven appeared to him and strengthened him' (Luke 22:43). If an angel could provide the support that Jesus needed at that moment, just think what God can do for you in moments of immense need. I don't believe we could ever be in greater need than he was then.

Sometimes angels get involved in service which is so down-to-earth that it makes you wonder why such an exotic heavenly being should stoop to such a mundane task. Take, for example, their care of Elijah. Elijah had won a victory over the prophets of Baal. Nothing those prophets could do, neither yelling to their god nor demonstrating their devotion by slashing themselves, did any good in bringing fire down on their altar. Enter Elijah. He douses God's altar with buckets of water, and then asks God to get the sacrifice burning. Woosh! Instant fire!

Unfortunately the day didn't end quite so victoriously. The fiery Queen Jezebel not only refused Elijah entry to the palace and access to King Ahab, but she decreed that Elijah should be killed. Now you would think that after such a victory at the altar, Elijah would have stormed the palace, challenged Jezebel and called down the judgment of God on this evil woman.

Surprise, surprise! Elijah is suddenly terrified of Jezebel, and runs for his life – all the way to Beer Sheba, the most southern city in Judah, and then on a further day's journey into the desert. He eventually comes to rest under a broom tree. He is candid enough to tell God exactly how he feels. 'I have had enough, Lord,' he says. 'Take my life.' He lies down under the tree and falls asleep.

This totally exhausted, drained servant of God has just resigned. God decides, however, that his basic needs should be taken care of before there was any heavy counselling for his spiritual condition. You can guess who he sent along to take care of Elijah's needs. 'All at once an angel touched him and said, "Get up and eat." He looked around, and there by his head was a cake of bread baked over hot coals, and a jar of water. He ate and drank and then lay down again' (1 Kgs. 19:5, 6).

God in his infinite care and understanding sent an angel to take care of his wounded servant. Have you ever felt like that? Have you ever said to the Lord that you have had enough, because you've given every ounce of energy you have, and got nowhere? That he might as well end your life here and now, because it's all useless? Have you ever reached a point of total exhaustion after irregular sleep patterns and inadequate eating habits? If you have, then take heart. There is absolutely no reason why God cannot meet your needs and mine. He could do it in the same way as he did for Elijah.

Messengers

Rather than intervene directly, angels are sometimes sent from heaven to earth to bring messages to us. As heavenly telegram messengers they have kept God's people from danger on many occasions. The classic example of this has to be the angelic messenger who appeared to Joseph in a dream. '"Get up," he said, "take the child and his mother and escape to Egypt. Stay there until I tell you, for Herod is going to search for the child to kill him"' (Matt. 2:13).

God doesn't let his plans be spoiled by powerful evil people. If it was necessary for Jesus's security to be safeguarded by angelic messengers, I think we can safely assume that God would use someone from the same department to safeguard us too when required.

I am sure angels must be very polite and deferential about who takes what messages. But there must have been a real flutter amongst the angels when one was chosen to tell Mary that she was to be the highly favoured mother of the Messiah. 'You will be with child and give birth to a son, and you are to give him the name Jesus' (Luke 1:32). The angel would have known that of all the messages angels would ever give to men and women on earth, this one was utterly unique – the Saviour of the world was to be born. Mary responds with great faith in the simple statement, 'I am the Lord's servant, may it be to me as you have said.'

So angels have important assignments in delivering messages to us earth brothers and sisters. If you are wondering how the business turned out with Mary, read Matthew 1. Joseph obviously didn't believe Mary's story about seeing an angel and he had decided to go for a quiet divorce when, yes, you've guessed it, an angel came to see him. In fact, the wonderful heartwarming events of the first Christmas are liberally laced with the activities of angels.

A little later in Acts, another event specifically mentions an angel. Arrogant King Herod delivers a public address, and the people praise him as being 'the voice of a god', not of a mere mortal. 'Immediately, because Herod did not give praise to God, an angel of the Lord struck him down, and he was eaten by worms and died' (Acts 12:23).

Angelic intervention

Until recently I always assumed that when I prayed, the answer would come by direct action of God through his Holy Spirit, or by moving other Christians to provide for those needs. It is only recently I have realised that God may use angels as well. For 'Are not all angels ministering spirits sent to serve those who will inherit salvation?' (Heb. 1:14).

It seems that angels have also a guardian role to play. Jesus made it quite plain that children are VIPs in his view of things. 'See that you do not look down on one of these little ones. For I tell you that their angels in heaven always see the face of my Father in heaven' (Matt. 18:10).

Maybe the reason we have never taken guardian angels particularly seriously is that they aren't very often obvious. You know how some people quietly get on with a job and you don't even realise that they are there? Well, I think maybe angels can operate a little like that. We should not be surprised at this, because the Bible warns us that angels sometimes operate in disguise. Hebrews urges Christian folk to be a little more hospitable: 'Do not forget to entertain strangers, for by so doing some people have entertained angels without knowing it' (Heb. 13:2). I'm not sure whether the writer was thinking of celebrated Old Testament cases, or maybe it was something that happened in the early church and has not been recorded for us. Anyway, the writer of Hebrews knew angels can work undercover.

For example, there is the angel that my cousin met in Canada. On a bluff looking down over the Fraser River which lazily makes its way to Vancouver lives my cousin Justyn Rees. Justyn is an evangelist and, with his team, takes the gospel to unchurched people all over Canada. He told me recently of a most extraordinary, unlikely angel, drafted in to take care of an emergency situation.

Early one morning Justyn left home for an appointment miles away, and soon reached an unguarded railway crossing a quiet stretch of road. He had never seen a train on this railway line. Although drivers should stop anyway, and check for trains, he was in a hurry and didn't even slow down. That is, he hadn't planned to, until he suddenly noticed a dog emerge from the side of the road. Annoyed that he couldn't keep going at a good speed, Justyn touched the brakes to slow a little but then found he had to do an emergency stop because the dog didn't cross the road quickly enough. By this time he was only a few yards from the railway crossing. His car screeched to a halt and in fact just touched the dog which was now standing still in front of him in the road. At the very moment the car came to a standstill, a huge locomotive appeared as from nowhere and rolled across the road on the railway lines only yards away.

If the dog had not stopped Justyn's car by standing in the road, he would certainly have been on the crossing as the train came. 'Did you know that angels can have fur and four legs?' Justyn remarked to me as he finished the story. I believe they can. One was certainly on guard duty that day.

Angels are at work for us now in a thousand ways, but mostly we aren't aware of them. God is very good in giving us a hint of what is happening in the unseen, by letting his secret agents enter our visible world from time to time. But if you are fortunate enough to experience God's goodness in this way, beware. Paul had to warn Christians of his day not to worship angels. In our world, so fascinated by the paranormal, we need to keep things in perspective. Angels would be horrified if we were to take an undue interest in them and their activities. I am sure they want us to focus our energy, attention and praise in the same direction as themselves: day and night giving praise to God and serving him.

Knowing that God has his secret agents working constantly on our behalf is a great thing. If God answers your prayers through a dramatic intervention by one of his angels, it wonderfully demonstrates his generosity in lending heaven's resources to earth. It will also encourage our faith. You would think it odd however, if you saw a group of people standing around at a signpost at the edge of the road, and admiring it. Signposts are put there to help us on our way to a destination.

Lucifer and the fallen angels

The spiritual world is not one of angels with harps snuggling into clouds, but one of spiritual warfare between good and evil forces. The Bible, of course, has a great deal to say about this spiritual conflict. It even reports on conversations between the Lord and Satan. No, I haven't dreamed that up. It is straight out of the book of Job. 'One day the angels came to present themselves before the Lord, and Satan also came with them. The Lord said to Satan, "Where have you come from?" Satan answered the Lord, "From roaming through the earth and going to and fro in it"' (Job 1:6, 7). Activities of this kind were never part of *my* childhood picture of heaven. But the Bible gives us a picture of God's sphere of operations, with his secret agents bringing reports to him, and even discussions about particular individuals on planet earth and negotiations with the enemy. Read the rest of Job 1 and you'll see what I mean.

Angels were created good, but with free will. It seems that all was well until Lucifer, one of God's most glorious created beings, rebelled against his creator. Isaiah 14:12–15 tells us something about it. Whatever can have led to such a thing happening? We aren't told the whole story, but we do know that when Lucifer fell, he took many angels with him. Perhaps there were promises of a new 'kingdom'. Perhaps he used exactly the same tactics as he did with Eve, casting doubts on God's genuine care and concern for all created beings. Some commentators even put a figure on the number of angels who rebelled – they reckon about one-third of the total.

So Lucifer became the permanent focus of all that was anti-God. As Satan, the devil, he has been the leader of all the fallen angels (demons) ever since. It seems there was no way back after this decision time. And for the angels who remained God's faithful servants, it seems that their chosen delight to do God's will is now irrevocably their destiny, without further decisions to be made. So let's dwell on the positive for a while. What events will take place between now and the time when we join those faithful angels?

8

The Countdown

Today you and I live on planet earth. One day we shall be with Jesus in heaven having said goodbye to time as we know it. What can we expect to happen between now and then? The Bible doesn't give all the answers but there's certainly plenty to be going on with.

The Second Coming

One day Jesus will return to earth, but this time he will not veil his divinity. He will come in power and might. Paul doesn't pretend that all the curtains on this have been drawn back. The mystery remains. But one thing is for sure: there will be a mega blast of heavenly trumpets, and then it will happen. Quick as blinking your eye, Christ will return in glory, claim his own, and we shall all be changed. The perishable has reached its sell-by date and off it goes. The new model appears out of nowhere and away we go. 'For the Lord himself will come down from heaven, with a loud command, with the voice of the archangel and with the trumpet call of God, and the dead in Christ will rise first' (1 Thess. 4:16).

When I was a child I used to worry that I'd wake up one morning and find no one else in the house. My fear was that Jesus might come back, take everyone else in the family off to heaven because they were so much better than me, and leave me behind. I really needn't have worried. I don't think anyone will sleep through the archangel's loud shout and the heavenly trumpeters doing their bit.

Peter has a go at a description of it in 2 Peter 3:10: 'But the day of the Lord will come like a thief. The heavens will disappear with a roar; the elements will be destroyed by fire, and the earth and everything in it will be laid bare.' The day he refers to is the same one mentioned in Isaiah 13:10. It is a time when God's judgment and blessing finally fall decisively on nations and individuals. It will come suddenly and unexpectedly. No one knows when a thief will come.

Fire and brimstone?

The apocalyptic language of destruction, roaring and fire has caused people to argue about how much is literal and how much is figurative. I remember Stuart Briscoe once confessing that when he'd first read this, he wrote off Peter's comments as coming from an uneducated fisherman. Then one day he opened a paper and saw a picture of a mushroom-like cloud in the sky. It was the atomic bomb at Hiroshima. He read of the bomb's capacity for unbelievable destruction. He then put the paper down and opened his Bible at 2 Peter 3. He read it again and believed what Peter had written is possible.

Whatever your interpretation of the picture is, Peter certainly wants us to know that God is going to wrap up the earth as we have known it and has promised us a new-look earth. And the new heavens are placed alongside this by Peter as part of a whole package which obviously ushers in a new era. Peter continues: 'But in keeping with his promise we are looking forward to a new heaven and new earth, the home of righteousness.'

That great blast of angelic trumpets will be the signal. We shall be scrambling over one another in our eagerness to get into our resurrection bodies.

Final judgment

The awful reality, of course, is that we have to accept the terrible flip-side to all this joy. The new heavens and new earth are going to be so wonderful because everything evil has been purged. I have hardly touched on this at all because I find it almost too awful to contemplate. However, Jesus states judgment as a certainty, not just a possibility.

Punishment is the inevitable result of sin, not just a maybe. Eternal separation from God is the guaranteed fate of those who reject the gift of eternal life. This is why it is so hard to even think about it. Jesus left us in no doubt that the worst kind of human suffering you and I have ever seen will be nothing compared with the awfulness of that day. Whether you depict it as crowds of screaming, distraught people, or silent suffering heaviness with numberless people whose heads are in their hands, no picture is adequate. The terror of final separation from a God who is love and is the source of all that is good and beautiful has got to be the worst spectre a human soul can contemplate.

In describing the scene in his own words, Jesus said that God will say to individual people, 'Depart from me, you who are cursed, into the eternal fire prepared for the devil and his angels . . . then they will go away to eternal punishment' (Matt. 25: 41, 46).

This is hell – the eternal fire that inevitably waits for that old rebel, the devil and all the one-time angels, turned demons, who followed him. And hell is not just for them, but for those individuals who through the course of their lives consciously or unconsciously followed in the same direction. Like the rich man who lived in luxury every day and gave no thought to the beggar at his gate, these are people who put number one first. The daily habit has turned into a destiny. 'I was hungry and you gave me nothing to eat, I was thirsty and you gave me nothing to drink, I was a stranger and you did not invite me in, I needed clothes and you did not clothe me, I was sick and in prison and you did not look after me' (Matt. 25: 42, 43). All this is a powerful motivation to action. Jesus's harshest words were directed at those who claimed a faith but whose lives showed no evidence of it. Jesus called them 'actors' (hypocrites). Beliefs that are not part of a changed lifestyle are obviously no beliefs at all. A. W. Tozer in *The Divine Conquest* (Fleming H. Revell Co., 1950) wrote about what he called the 'true quality of faith': 'It invariably effects radical transformation in the life of the one who exercises it. It shifts the inward gaze from self to God. It introduces its possessor into the life of heaven upon earth.' The whole book of James questions whether the kind of faith that doesn't result in a changed life is in fact real, Christian, saving faith at all.

The first job I did when I graduated with a degree in economics was to work for a firm of chartered accountants as an auditor. I spent my days with a team of people checking up on whether firms' and companies' accounts and accounting procedures complied with the law. We didn't take anyone's word for it. We had a whole procedure to follow to check out whether what people said they were doing was actually happening. I have often discovered since that I need to do a regular audit on myself. Not checking up on my finances so much as making sure I am doing what I say I am doing. That I am believing what I say I believe. That I am walking the talk. Trusting in Christ is a lifestyle, not simply a belief. Matthew 25 proves that a personal audit could be a very helpful thing. We are certainly going to face a giant audit one day. The reality is that there is a deadline date for many audits and necessary adjustments. After that it's too late.

However we picture this great and terrible day, nothing can ever adequately convey the horror it will truly be as millions of people realise the awful mistake they have made in following their feelings instead of God's commands; following the things that the devil made sure were bright and attractive, instead of the slightly less brightly painted but much more secure ways of godliness and holiness; in living for the moment rather than thinking of eternity.

The Holy Spirit makes sure that we have intimations of these things. Our consciences prod us and remind us from time to time. But for those who deliberately ignore the gentle wooing of the Spirit and the anxious voice of conscience, and turn their back on Christ knowingly, there will come an awful day when *their choice* to live without God will be given to them. It will be final. No appeal. No way back. A terrible day.

Gathering people together for a judgment is pictured by John in Revelation. In a scene rather like Jesus's parable of the wheat and tares growing together till harvest time and then being gathered up and separated, John sees the angels out with their harvesting machinery. 'Take your sharp sickle and gather the clusters of grapes from the earth's vine, because its grapes are ripe' (Rev. 14:17).

103

Then the angel uses his divine cutting tool to gather up the harvest on earth and he throws this into 'the great winepress of God's wrath' (verse 19). We may have wondered how people get away with the evil they do. They don't. We will reap what we have sown.

I really want to get off this subject as soon as I can, but I think if we're to be honest rather than escapist, we must face the fact of a final judgment. Revelation has many pictures of this. One depicts an angel as God's agent sending down an awesome missive of terror from heaven to earth. 'The angel took the censer, filled it with fire from the altar, and hurled it on the earth' (Rev. 8:5). This is followed by awesome thunder, lightning and an earthquake.

I don't know if ever you have allowed your imagination to roam over what a full-scale nuclear war would be like. Nevil Shute's novel, *On the Beach*, describes the consequences of a nuclear exchange between world superpowers and the horrific effect on daily lives of individuals, and I was gripped. I remained involved with the characters of the story for weeks afterwards. It was a dreadful book to read in one sense, but it made me realise that the terror of the full force of God's judgment must be infinitely greater than the awful experience of the worst destruction man can invent.

Such frightening things are probably not intended for us to dwell on morbidly, but neither are they to be ignored. I'm sure that angels must rejoice in heaven whenever we rediscover the urgency of our situation, and of the reality of the coming last judgment. It can be a powerful motivating force, causing us to fall on our knees and plead with God for our friends and neighbours. It should drive out our apathy, and propel us into involvement with people so that we can communicate all the good things God has for them if only they will turn to him.

So don't ignore the evidence, says Peter. By the same spoken word of God 'the present heavens and earth are reserved for fire, being kept for the day of judgment and destruction of the ungodly' (2 Pet. 3:7). Peter does not want us to think that the passage of time makes the promises of God any less relevant. God will do what he has said he will do.

Another millennium

There is another important job which an angel will carry out at the end of time. 'And I saw an angel coming down out of heaven, having the key to the Abyss and holding in his hand a great chain' (Rev. 20:1). What a great day that will be! A specially appointed angel will lock up the devil for a period that John describes as a thousand years or a millennium. After a brief period of freedom when he goes about his usual business of deceiving people and fighting good, the devil is then despatched where he can do no more harm 'for ever and ever' (Rev. 20:10).

New heavens and a new earth?

God has promised that at the end of the world, 'Behold I will create new heavens and a new earth' (Isa. 65:17). The heavens and the earth, which Genesis 1 tells us God made, are now on a limited lease and are going to be made new.

I always assumed that God would one day blow up the whole of his original creation, so that it all vanished, just as miraculously as he brought it into being. I was brought up on the Authorised Version, and its vivid phrase, 'the earth also and the works that are therein shall be burned up' led me for many years to assume that the whole of this present earth was going to go up one day with a colossal bang, just as some people think that the whole universe started with one big bang. I saw pictures in the paper of mushroom-shaped clouds from megaton atomic explosions and thought that maybe one day God was going to allow man to invent a bomb big enough to blow up the whole earth.

This idea always left me with a very funny feeling. If everything that I have known, experienced and can relate to is not going to be around any more, how do I even begin to think of what heaven will be like? If there is nothing from my previous experience to link it on to, I should have to close my eyes and do the best I can to dream up something which is entirely different. And not being a terribly imaginative sort, the best that I have ever been able to come up with was a misty hazy picture of me floating around, somewhat like a ghost in a sun-drenched happy sky scene. Only I wasn't allowed to think of the sun or clouds or anything I know in this way of thinking, because it's all going to be blown into little pieces and vanish. It's no wonder I had trouble picturing what my life would be like after this one. The one thing I could come back to with certainty was that Jesus would be there and because of that everything would be great.

Since then, my ideas have changed. Now I think that perhaps this world will be renewed, and so become the 'new earth'. If you want to think more about the future heaven and earth having a more earthly aspect than you might have expected, read David Lawrence's eye-opening book, *Heaven: It's Not the End of the World!* (Scripture Union). I found his thinking very constructive and biblical. His *pièce de résistance* is to quote Jesus's beatitude from Matthew 5:5: 'Blessed are the meek, for they will inherit the earth.' This is actually Jesus quoting from Psalm 37:11, but the Old Testament verse has the word 'land' rather than 'earth'. It looks very much as though Jesus is wanting us to grasp the idea that the Jews' expectation of returning to a land was small-scale thinking. God is thinking big, and plans for all his people to be living happily ever after on a *renewed earth*.

So I think that for years I misunderstood the passages in the Bible about the new heaven and the new earth. I now no longer envisage a total annihilation of all that God originally made. Rather I see the new thing that God will do as being a purifying, redeeming and restructuring of the universe that he originally created out of nothing. This is a very different picture because it means all the best things that you and I have experienced and can relate to will go on.

Lawrence quotes theologians from N. T. Wright and G. C. Berkouwer to A. Koberle and John Stott. I must confess I find it very convincing stuff. We shall never know all the answers. But God has created an amazing world and to purify, cleanse and redeem his creation is a very appealing approach to me. I think this is a wonderful picture. Jesus comes back to earth and the 'old order of things has passed away . . . I am making everything new!' (Rev. 21:4, 5).

I had a real treat at the cinema recently. It was no ordinary film, but a 3-D experience. As we went into the auditorium we were given a special pair of glasses. We took our seats and waited. When the lights went down and the performance began I put the fancy spectacles on. I nearly leapt out of my seat. All of a sudden the flat screen came out at me as if the whole scene was quite literally happening three-dimensionally on some kind of vast platform that reached right up to the edge of my seat. The evening's entertainment explored the beauties of nature in a way I'd never seen before. Brightly coloured flowers were so real and large I actually reached out and tried to touch them. There were mountains with snow so crisp and dazzling I gasped at their wonder. I think our appreciation of the renewed wonders of God's creation will be something like that, just like putting on a pair of those amazing spectacles. We knew it was wonderful before, but suddenly the appreciation will be magnified a million times.

Can you imagine what it would be like to see our dirty, polluted old planet earth as God meant it to be – just as it was in the Garden of Eden? Amazing colour and beauty – the taints of sin are swept away and we get a whole new and beautiful present of God's creation. All this could be regarded as fanciful if the same themes did not occur elsewhere in the New Testament. It seems to me that they don't just 'occur', but actually develop as the New Testament unfolds.

Travelling a little further in the New Testament, the idea of a redeemed earth appears to run into trouble in Peter's second letter. In his third chapter he sets out by telling you and me his aim 'to stimulate you to wholesome thinking' (2 Pet. 3:1). He goes on to tell us that 'earth and everything in it will be laid bare (2 Pet. 3:10). But I don't think God regards the beautiful earth he created as disposable. So perhaps Peter's comments can be read a different way. He mentions the earth being cleaned up from evil influences by the flood. In the next breath he goes on to tell us that the same God will give the order for the *cleansing* of the earth by fire. I have no doubt there are some people who would argue that this means the end of our present earth and God creating something different. Personally I think that to take this as a fire of purification rather than annihilation makes more sense in this context. I also find it a more helpful picture in fitting things into the overall jigsaw puzzle of how everything will slot together as God's great big plans unfold.

I am intrigued too by the fact that Peter talks about 'the present heavens' as well as the earth needing a fiery clean up. It seems as though he is including all the unseen spiritual realms where, as we know, there are evil spirits as well as angels going about their work. It isn't hard to see that the earth needs a fiery cleansing by the 'destruction of the ungodly'. Unseen, but nevertheless real also, are the heavenly realms. It all seems to make sense, too, in the way Peter pictures the situation after the clean-up. 'In keeping with his promise we are looking forward to a new heaven and a new earth, the home of righteousness' (2 Pet. 3:13).

David Lawrence has a significant comment on this which I found really helpful.

It is important to note that the creation of a new earth will be different from the creation of the earth on which we now live in one vital respect. A clue to the difference lies in the use of the Greek words *kainos* and *neos*. Both are translated in English as 'new'; *kainos* denotes 'that which is better than the old', whereas *neos* is used for 'that which has not yet been, that which has just made its appearance'. (*Heaven: It's Not the End of the World!*)

When God first made the earth, it was *neos*. It had never existed; it was not a new model based on an old pattern; God created it out of nothing . . . however, according to Peter and to John (Rev. 21:1) our future is to be spent on a *kainos* earth – an earth that is a new improved version of the one that has already existed.' (Colin Brown (ed.), *The New International Dictionary of New Testament Theology* vol. II, Paternoster Press, 1976)

The heavenly banquet

A picture of our future as a heavenly banquet is found in the book of Revelation. Many, many books have been written trying to understanding this amazing book with its many prophecies, so all I will add is the comment that whatever this 'heavenly banquet' entails, the whole wonderful purpose of the wedding supper of the lamb will be to enjoy the presence of Jesus and to worship and celebrate with him. Certainly the Bible's prophecies concerning the future include some wonderful celebration meals. If you want to get to know new neighbours or have a good time with old friends, what do you do? You invite them round for a meal. All through the centuries, eating and drinking with those you know best has been a sign of friendship.

We may think of some of the Bible pictures as simply being a mechanism for conveying an idea. However, I don't think Jesus's disciples would have been thinking that way when they listened round the table at the last supper: 'I tell you the truth, I will not drink again of the fruit of the vine until that day when I drink it anew in the kingdom of God' (Mark 14:25). Not so many days later Jesus was eating breakfast with them on a lakeside beach in his resurrection body; deliberately taking a piece of boiled fish and eating it in full view so that they could see he was real and not a ghost. So why not a real meal with heavenly wine in the new heavens and new earth of the kingdom of God? It would certainly fit in with

Isaiah's vision of the new heavens and new earth, where he sees us building houses and living in them, planting vineyards and eating their fruit (Isa. 65:21).

Since some of the best times of human interaction, conversation and celebration take place over mealtimes, I can't help thinking that in the new age to come we shall have some great times around the meal table. Who would you like to invite to your heavenly dinner party?

The new Jerusalem

John also has his turn at pointing the way to what things will be like:

> Then I saw a new heaven and a new earth, for the first heaven and the first earth had passed away, and there was no longer any sea. I saw the Holy City, the new Jerusalem, coming down out of heaven for God, prepared as a bride beautifully dressed for her husband. (Rev. 21:1, 2)

The language problem may perhaps be something to encourage us rather than depress us. Haven't you ever felt feelings so deep they are inexpressible? Haven't you ever said, 'I am lost for words' at a time when something very big has happened? So don't ever make the kind of remark that I once heard said: 'I am not sure I am looking forward to heaven too much – streets of gold don't really appeal to me.' You will have a very embarrassing telling off from the apostle John if you say anything like that. He will make us feel awfully dim as he tries to point out that he was simply using the best of the finite to tackle the impossible and describe the infinite.

111

If you ever saw the film *The Shaw Shank Redemption*, you'll recall that it contains a wonderful illustration of this. (In case you did see the movie, I should like you to know that I wasn't impressed by some of the language, and that I walked out during a couple of violent scenes.) The story is set in a tough American prison with dozens of men serving life sentences. The prison regime is shown as oppressive and corrupt. Life sentences seem to mean life, as they did in the fifties and sixties. The gradual dehumanisation of each man becomes apparent.

Andy McFay is a man convicted of murder who is in fact innocent and is determined not to be dehumanised by the system. On one memorable day, Andy somehow obtains a record of a piece of Italian opera. Breaking all the rules, he plays the music over the public address system throughout the whole prison. There is a moving few minutes whilst our hero sits beside the record, eyes closed, drinking in the beauty. Outside in the prison yard dozens of hardened criminals stop whatever they are doing and stand absolutely still looking up at the loudspeaker. An unlikely audience in blue prison garb is captured by a sound which reaches deep into the soul.

When the music dies away a prison-hardened old black lifer comments that he didn't know what it was 'those two Italian ladies were singing about, but it had to be something so beautiful that it was out of this world'.

We don't have to understand all the language. Our spirit has the capacity to pick up the deep communication of realities too big for our brains but so important for our souls.

Walking the Holy City

An angel gives John a guided tour of the city later on in Revelation. This includes getting out his tape measure to find out exactly how big the city is. And it is big! To be precise, 1,400 miles from one end to the other. Then another 1,400 miles from one side to the other and – here is the exciting bit – 1,400 miles high (a new dimension to living?). That of course makes it a perfect cube and therein lies a lot of significance. Perhaps most significant of all, it is just like the most holy place of the tabernacle and the temple – a perfect cube, a perfect and complete place.

Another thing the angel measured was the thickness of the walls: about 200 feet. I live in a house which is a converted barn. The oldest part is around three hundred years old. The walls in this area are nearly 3 feet thick, and I have several times remarked to friends that modern houses perhaps aren't quite built to the same solid standard. But who needs walls more than sixty times thicker than my house has? I suppose if one is thinking of longevity, you could say that if my walls have stood for three hundred years, this new Jerusalem is certainly going to make it for about twenty thousand years. But then, of course, we're out of time and into eternity, so we wouldn't even notice a few thousand years passing.

No, I think John has in mind the purpose of a wall: security. And very important it was back in those times. We still see the same principle in today's world. There is a wealthy man who lives on a road I frequently drive along. His beautiful house is surrounded by high brick walls topped with barbed wire. He wants to keep undesirables out so that he can feel secure inside.

The most chilling and impressive example of security I have seen was on a recent visit to Belfast. My host, Noel Hunter, took me on a tour of the city. I had seen it on TV but the reality was a shock. We passed numerous police stations totally enclosed in colossal high brick walls. There were army checkpoints with every conceivable device. We stopped at a traffic light where there was a barrier across the road and a strange-looking reinforced building towered above us. I could just make out a uniformed figure inside. 'He will be checking my car registration on his computer,' Noel told me. 'Security.' From behind the protection of his huge brick wall the uniformed figure pressed a button, the traffic lights turned green and the barrier was raised. We were crossing from a Protestant to a Catholic area. The road ran along the so-called 'peace line'. Huge brick walls on each side of the road separated Catholic from Protestant communities. It was all a matter of security.

So we still have the same basic problems as societies of earlier days, and city walls are still in use today to keep undesirables out, and give some sense of security to those within. John must have wanted to give us a massive sense of the secure place in which we would be in the new order of things. Nothing bad is ever going to penetrate heaven. Everyone there will never have any fears about their personal safety – certainly not in a physical sense but not in any emotional or spiritual sense either. We shall feel utterly safe. John tells us 'there will be no more death or mourning or crying or pain, for the old order of things has passed away' (Rev. 21:4).

The death of a marriage partner, the death of a child or someone else close to you is a heartbreaking experience. Those of us who have experienced any of these things will know just how liberating it will be to be assured that nothing like that will ever happen in heaven. Those of us who have never experienced these things may well be stalked by the fear that they might happen. The process of death itself for some people can be an ugly thing, even though it opens the gateway to new life. The deep ache which accompanies these experiences can surprise us with its intensity. Time and again, I have felt myself and heard other people say, 'Surely life was never meant to be like this!' The sorrows, sadness and traumas of life often happen to people who we feel are innocent victims. They seem to deserve something better and this sparks a sense of outrage in us. Sometimes we may rage against God and tell him, 'This is unfair!' Sometimes we may just silently weep at the burden and hurt of the process of life.

But all these things will be gone, together with the mourning and grieving which accompanies them. Whatever else does not seem clear from the picture language of the Bible about heaven, this bit of Revelation seems to me as clear as daylight and I love it! I think it rings bells with something deep down in the soul.

As well as the description of the Holy City as a secure and complete place, the new world John sees in Revelation 21 has some negatives described in verses 22 to 27. When I first read them they rather surprised me because they are the kind of positive things that you really like to have around on planet earth – especially if you are a Christian.

The first one is that there are no churches in heaven. 'I did not see a temple in the city.' What, no churches? All those seminar hours invested in church growth and church planting courses have come to nothing?! There are no churches because we will not need them in heaven. John tells us that there is no temple 'because the Lord God Almighty and the Lamb are its (the city's) temple'.

The temple in Bible times was a place set apart for God. In earlier times, the holy of holies was a place where God's presence was especially known by a chosen few. Since the curtain into the most holy place was ripped open, at the resurrection of Jesus, things have changed.

The way to God is open. Anyone can know him by the presence of his Holy Spirit any time, anywhere. In heaven that process will be taken one stage further. Jesus will be there, known and visible all the time.

Now for another word from John. 'The city does not need the sun or the moon to shine on it.' No more gentle spring sunshine on delicate snowdrops in an English garden? No more basking on a beautiful beach in the blazing sun? And what about the moon? Maybe you had a clear picture in your mind of one of those nights when the full moon bathed a countryside scene with light so clear it was almost like day – but because it was night it was extra beautiful. Sue had a little girl at our home recently who is a near neighbour. Walking out of our front door with her, in the evening, Sue looked up at the glorious full moon. 'Isn't that beautiful?' she commented. 'Yes, it's lovely,' replied the little girl. 'You know, we've got a beautiful moon like that at our house too.' Gabby was too young to realise it was the same moon but she certainly knew it was beautiful.

However, John is almost certainly talking in figurative language. He gives us the reason for his statement that the new city does not need a sun or moon: 'for the glory of God gives it light and the Lamb is its lamp.' I wouldn't mind betting if I asked you to picture Jesus or one of his angels appearing to you, somewhere in your description you would include something about a very bright light. Certainly when God appeared to Saul and spoke to him, 'suddenly a light from heaven flashed around him' (Acts 9:3). Jesus said 'I am the light of the world' (John 8:12). So perhaps it is no surprise to find John visualising heaven with the bright light of Jesus shining everywhere. To have the power and energy of the all-powerful Creator present with us will be blazingly glorious. If this is something bigger than the combined energy of the sun and moon – and it is – then forget ideas of the most powerful dark glasses to ease the glare on your eyes; this is something way beyond our imagining.

The angel is coming to the end of his guided tour of the city. He shows John 'the river of the water of life'. Some of my happiest memories are associated with rivers. Fishing on the banks of the River Rother with my brother when I was a small boy growing up on our farm. A bright crisp day around Easter sailing on the Norfolk Broads with some teenage school friends as herons flapped lazily past. Punting on the river in Oxford past the majestic old colleges with noisy ducks round us. Sitting back on cushions while my family rowed me up a beautiful stretch of the Medway near our home for a picnic in a grassy field on my fiftieth birthday. And here is the river of the water of life!

Jesus urged the Samaritan woman at the well to ask him for a drink of the 'living water'. He describes it as 'water which will quench your thirst for ever', so that whoever drinks it will never need to drink again. And promises more than that: 'the water I give will become a spring of water welling up to eternal life' (John 4:14). Isaiah addresses 'all you who are thirsty' (Isa. 55:1), using water as a symbol of spiritual refreshment. The psalmist likens those who delight in the Lord to 'trees planted by streams of water, which yield their fruit in season and whose leaves do not wither. Whatever they do prospers' (Ps. 1:3).

So God has the kind of water which satisfies us. Being beside flowing water seems to provide for all our needs and put us on the right road to a fruitful life of success for God. No wonder the same picture is used of heaven by John. There will be no thirst unsatisfied there. There will be no sense of the dissatisfaction of being unfruitful for God. If rivers and water give us any kind of picture of happiness, serenity and satisfaction, then the real thing is certainly going to far outshine the picture.

Reconciling the nations

The angel's guided sightseeing tour also includes a look at the 'tree of life' standing beside the river. Here again there is more good news. 'The leaves of the tree are for the healing of the nations' (Rev. 22:2). As we are assailed day by day with reports from trouble spots around the world, I find myself struggling to visualise a new heaven and earth where all the nations are healed. Over the past few decades there has been an average of more than twenty major trouble spots around the world where there is either international conflict or violence between different groups of people within the same nation. Every time you open a newspaper, listen to the radio or watch the TV, the news industry ensures that we hear every depressing detail about the worst of human nature.

For me the trouble spots are not too far away, either. On Friday 9 February 1996 at 7.01 p.m. the IRA detonated a massive bomb at South Quay, Canary Wharf, London, killing two teenage boys and causing millions of pounds worth of damage. This is only a few miles from my home and I travel to London regularly. Within my own country, healing between two groups of people looks as illusive and impossible as ever. Please don't think I am a pessimist. I believe I have seen at least one national miracle – in April 1994. Who predicted a smooth and peaceful transition from white minority to black majority rule in South Africa? But perhaps the bigger question is, has there been permanent healing? Will all the abuse and violence of the past be forgiven and forgotten? Many of us who love Africa wait with prayerful baited breath for the long-term outcome in the new South Africa. Please don't get me wrong. Every fair election, just peace treaty, and cease-fire is a wonderful thing. But attaining the lasting healing of nations and groups of people is something rather different.

It will happen in heaven. There will be no more reports of civil war or international unrest. Thousands of journalists will have to find new jobs! The kinds of impossible events which politicians, peace negotiators, endless resources and goodwill have failed to achieve throughout the history of this planet will become a reality in heaven. Working for peace on earth has to be one of the most worthwhile activities possible. However, to do so without reference to the God of heaven who will one day bring complete healing to nations, and who meanwhile can change human hearts (yes, in South Africa and in Northern Ireland), will sadly be only wasted effort.

One of the most powerful aspects of the perfect unity we can look foward to is that the curse of different languages which God used when he stepped in at the building of the Tower of Babel will no longer divide us. We shall all be given a new heavenly tongue. In the glorious gathering where every nation will be represented, all our cultural differences will be enriching rather than dividing. Mutual understanding and concern will dominate relationships. John's vision of a multi-national worship force will come true: 'I looked and there before me was a great multitude that no-one could count, from every nation, tribe, people and language, standing before the throne and in front of the Lamb' (Rev. 7:9).

The heavenly bride

This peaceful and harmonious place will also be a *very* beautiful place, as the angel intimates to John saying, 'Come, I will show you the bride, the wife of the Lamb', and taking him to a high mountain to see the Holy City coming down out of heaven (Rev. 21:9–10).

Any bride will go to endless trouble, and often a great deal of expense, to ensure that they are at their most beautiful on their wedding day. It was the same in John's day. Things haven't changed much. Have you noticed how people peer into any car with white wedding ribbons and how we tend to stop and stare if we happen to pass a wedding party just coming out of church? John's other picture for conveying ideas of beauty still holds true today.

As a recent wedding anniversary present, I secretly spirited Sue's engagement ring down to the local jeweller and asked him to give it a once-over and smarten it up. When I collected it a few days later, I was amazed. It was sitting on a small velvet-covered cushion on the jeweller's counter when I spotted it. I gasped as I picked it up and held it to the light. The diamonds and emeralds danced and sparkled in the sunlight. 'That's beautiful!' I breathed. I have to tell you that in fact the ring was not a very expensive one (I was born in Scotland so you could have guessed that), but it really is a very beautiful thing.

That is why John uses the picture of precious stones to convey something of the beauty of the place God is preparing for us. He says it has the brilliance of the glory of God, 'like that of a very precious jewel' (Rev. 21:11). To try and get our imagination going, he mentions as many precious stones as he can think of which the city is constructed from – jasper, crystal, sapphire, emerald, carnelian, chrysolite, topaz, amethyst plus gold and pearls and even one or two other precious stones which my commentary tells me cannot be identified. John is running away with himself in an attempt to get us to the heights of beauty.

Whatever you think of as the most beautiful thing imaginable – forget it! God's heaven is going to be a million times more beautiful.

Having got that far, it's not hard to see that John wants us to know that this new Holy City is *very* holy. If he is likening it to the most holy places he can think of and magnifying it a few thousand times in size, then he must be telling us that our feeble glimpses of holiness are going to be overtaken by what we will experience in heaven: a place set apart for God, where no sin of any kind spoils anything at all. 'Nothing impure will enter it, nor will anyone who does what is shameful or deceitful' (Rev. 21:27). John makes it clear in this verse that we shall never have to cringe at foul language, ache at infidelity, or experience the sinking feeling of wondering about motives others have towards us – everything will be wonderfully pure. All of the impurity, shame and deceit which is so much part of the fabric of the society in which we live, will be totally banished.

I can't wait!

9

The New Heaven and Earth

Creation will be renewed

As we saw at the end of the last chapter, the world we live in now is far from pure. Indeed, Paul pictures the *whole* of God's creation as infected by sin through decay and disease. The destructive forces in nature are attributed by Paul to the spoiling and corrupting effect of sin. In Romans 8 he paints a picture of human suffering and our longing to be rid of it all as it is swallowed up in the glory 'that will be revealed' (verse 18). Then Paul turns to creation. He declares that the whole natural universe 'waits in eager expectation' and in the hope that it 'will be liberated from its bondage to decay and brought into the glorious freedom of the children of God' (Rom. 8:19, 21).

Paul widens the scope of redemption to include *every-thing*. John tells us in the first chapter of his Gospel that there is nothing that exists in heaven or earth that was not made by Jesus, the Word of God. Paul reminds us of this in Colossians 1 and elaborates a little to make sure we understand that *everything* created in heaven or earth, visible and invisible, and every single power or ruler that exists, derives *everything* from him.

For God was pleased to have all his fulness dwell in him, and through him to reconcile to himself all things, whether things on earth or things in heaven, by making peace through his blood, shed on the cross. (Col. 1:19, 20)

Surely God has gone to such lengths in order to put right his malfunctioning creation, in order to restore it to its original perfection, rather than do away with it all? And yet, in the meantime the whole universe lives in an uneasy tension. Paul aptly describes this unease as 'groaning as in the pains of childbirth' and what's more, he says that we have this same tension within us. Christians also 'groan inwardly as we wait eagerly for our adoption, the redemption of our bodies' (Rom. 8:23). And this redemption *will* come. Everything that God has made will be wonderfully free from the terrible prison of decay and ruin. This seems to imply that the physical universe is not destined for destruction or annihilation, but for renewal.

That's why we look forward to the new heavens and new earth; that great dawning of a new era where the destruction and damage of a few thousand years of rebellion will be put straight. Heaven will be restored to its peace-filled original state. Earth will be redeemed from the decay that set in at the Fall, and the great big ball of God's total creation will roll on into a new and glorious future.

However much God delights in the glories of his hundreds of millions of stars and planets and the rest of the universe, planet earth is special. An evening I shall never forget was an occasion when Dr David Ingram stood at one end of our sitting-room and sketched an imaginary map of the entire universe on the wall behind him. Vice-chancellor of the University of Kent and a physicist, he held fifty of our neighbours and friends spellbound as he showed us the map. The end wall represented an area millions of light years across with billions of stars and planets littered in its vastness. But the red colouring which would represent the area particularly touched by God's love was a tiny one. He reached down to a particular point and pretended to put a tiny dot of red on one planet. And of course you've guessed where that was.

The Bible indicates that God's care and concern is concentrated on a tiny geographical area where his most treasured pinnacle of creation lives. With all the trouble he has taken over the whole course of the history of time to maintain that loving care and attention, I cannot believe that the new heavens and new earth will be anything other than a kind of amalgamation of God's dwelling-place and ours.

I find the most helpful way to picture the new life we shall live is as the kind of perfect harmony and closest friendship that we could possibly imagine between heaven and earth renewed. God's dwelling-place and ours united. God will still be God and we will be his creatures but heaven and earth merge, since the new redeemed earth is now a place where righteousness can feel at home.

But since God has been so good as to draw back the curtain a little and let us peep into the future, he has a purpose in it. Even if our glimpses of the gloriousness of the future are limited, they can still be transforming. Living in the light of what we know changes a lot of our perspectives. Many life experiences are transforming. Have you ever said to yourself, 'I shall never be the same after this.' A glimpse of heaven is like that.

A thing I had never noticed before was that the holy

city, the new Jerusalem, is to come *down* out of heaven from God to us. The whole idea of us floating off to heaven somewhere invisible seems to be reversed. It seems that it's a picture of God moving house, instead. The whole thing gives me a heartwarming picture of a God who previously has found earth just one colossal heartache 'moving in' to a renewed, cleansed and purified atmosphere, the home of righteousness.

The wonder of the new heavens and new earth is surely that the Creator God can now be at home again among his creation. His greatness and righteousness are not barred from a redeemed earth by the shop-soiled taints which previously made things impossible. It seems as though heaven and earth are reunited. Creator and creation can walk hand in hand. The Garden of Eden is restored – people and their God in happy friendship enjoying his creation. Isn't that heaven?

What about those we love?

Marriage is for life. But love is an eternal thing. If you are happily married, you've probably wondered whether you and your loved one will we be able to stop in a nice place for a quiet chat in heaven, or will rush past each other, so busy with heavenly chores that you may not even recognise one another, may not feel the need to stop and talk, or, worse still, might wish you could be close again like it was on earth. It doesn't just apply to marriage. Relationships of real caring touch us at our deepest points. They are the happiest things on earth. What will they be like in heaven?

Jesus answered a question about marriage in heaven in Matthew 22:30. After the resurrection, there is no more marriage, but we are 'like the angels in heaven'.

Obviously the exclusive relationship that marriage creates is an institution just for this life. Every marriage service reminds us that God created it first for comfort and companionship; and second for the propagation of the species.

But does that mean that you will not recognise your partner in heaven? That the actual relationship will not exist any more? If relationships are creations of God, then surely rather than being destroyed in heaven, they will be much much better. Different – but better. The crippling effects of suspicion or mistrust will be gone. A joyful openness will free the shyest person.

What about those special friendships? What about some situations that, viewed from planet earth, seem potentially embarrassing? (My father-in-law keeps asking me what he is going to say to his first wife who died three years ago, now that he has married again.) I believe our earthly perspectives will be long, long forgotten. Since no hint of jealousy could exist in any heavenly relationship, the kind of exclusiveness that we reserve for special relationships here must be very different there. But it will happen in some extraordinary way that doesn't preclude our having special links with some people in a form that does not put others down or leave them out.

Heavenly rewards

Our village has a number of people who are retired. Most of them, after a lifetime of hard work, enjoy the rewards of their labours. For some the reward is a regular holiday in an exotic location. For others it is the peace and quiet of pottering in their country garden without the pressure of rushing out to work each day. To some extent the amount and quality of their rewards are linked to their abilities and how hard they have worked. It isn't therefore any great surprise to me to find that God also promises rewards to those who have been faithful and worked hard for him.

But let's just get one thing quite clear. Our entry into God's kingdom, with his wonderful salvation and promise of eternal life, is *not* one of those rewards we are talking about. Those things are a free gift purchased by Christ when he died on the cross and rose again. No amount of hard work or faithfulness from us will earn us those things.

But Jesus clearly talked about the kingdom of heaven having an element of reward. His parable of the talents in Matthew 25 hammers home the point that we are all responsible for the gifts God has given us and how we use them. And the outcome of our stewardship is not simply a matter of interest, but the deciding factor in the role we shall play in God's kingdom. The picture is of rewards given to those who use their gifts, adding their hard work and initiative to the natural endowments God has given them. Strangely, the rewards given in the parable are more responsibility and more work. But this is obviously not an onerous thing, because congratulations are offered with the words: 'Come and share your master's happiness!' (Matt. 25.23).

At the other end of the scale, the one who has a gift but does not use it, sitting on his hands and waiting for the master to return, is described as 'wicked and lazy'. I regret to say that my school reports sometimes included comments like 'could do much better with a little extra effort'. But there were redeeming moments. In one memorable high spot I was actually called into the hallowed presence of the headmaster, who congratulated me on being promoted to the rank of prefect (a reward involving further administrative responsibilities).

School isn't the only place where these kind of admonitions or accolades are handed out. Whether it's your superiors at work, the captain of your sporting team or the organiser of some other activity, all of us welcome the rewards and fear the reprimand. Jesus indicates that we have good reason to apply the same principles to the way we live our lives.

Paul makes this principle clear in 1 Corinthians 3. You and I are putting up some kind of an edifice with the activities of our lives. Paul makes it clear that there is only one foundation for life, Jesus Christ. But he goes on to tell us that once you have Jesus as your foundation, this isn't the end of the important choices of your life. Every day you and I make choices about how we spend our time, energy, money and effort. All this is building something. We're either investing our lives in something that will count for eternity, or we are spending the resources available to us on activities which make no dent in eternity. A life lived which leaves no vapour trail to point others to heaven is a wasted life. Who will then ever be quite literally 'eternally grateful' that our path crossed theirs?

The stuff of your life is being built into a building which one day will be tested by God. One day each person's 'work will be shown for what it is' (1 Cor. 3.13). Now of course Paul is not talking about the judgment fires of hell – because he has just spoken about this illustration applying to people who have Jesus Christ as their foundation stone. But what he is saying is that Christian people can do different things with their lives and what they do will be judged – and rewarded accordingly.

Paul lists various possible building materials: gold,

silver, costly stones, wood, hay or straw. Some of these materials will survive fire, and some will not. Some years ago when I first read these verses, an immediate picture popped into my head. In the hope you may find it helpful, here it is.

I picture each of us Christians waiting to go in and meet the Lord Jesus. As we sit around in a waiting room, before our name is called, each of us clutches something rather like a little doll's house. It is the building that represents all that we have built, each day of our lives. My name is called and I step up to where an angel ticks off the register. It could be the Lamb's Book of Life, for our names are all written there. Then with a kindly smile he indicates the mini-building I am holding and says, 'I just need to put that through the fire test before you go in to meet the Master.'

I hand my little building over the reception counter and the angel takes it a few feet away to where he has a sort of giant Bunsen burner going. Holding the precious creation of my life with the tips of his fingers he deftly passes it through the flame. When I'd stepped up to the desk I could feel that the heat of the flame was pretty intense, so anything passing right through it is going to get a real roasting. He has his back to me while he carries out this procedure, but as he turns to face me again, one of two things is possible. Either he will be holding a little doll's house which was made of durable materials that will survive a roasting in a fire. Or as he turns he will be empty-handed, because anything combustible he was holding will have been burnt to ashes. If he hands back something that has passed the fire test, it will be with a 'well done' and perhaps an explanation of the way the rewards system works in the kingdom of God. If he has nothing to hand back over the counter, I will still be invited to go on through the great big doors into that special place for my personal audience with the Master. The promise of being in his company is not at issue. But what a wonderful thing to have something to present to him! To know that whether or not others told me so on planet earth, *he* thinks I have done well.

Paul does make one thing abundantly clear. There will be some people in heaven whose life-work is burned up and worth nothing but somehow they will 'be saved, but only as one escaping through the flames' (1 Cor. 3:15). To be quite truthful, I find it quite hard to understand this illustration because faith without works is dead. But then I have met enough Christians who in my humble judgment are either lazy, not fully committed, compromised in some area or thinking of how they can save their life rather than lose it. And don't worry, I recognise a good deal of these awful weaknesses in myself. But there it is. We are promised rewards. Our work will be shown for what it is. God's pure daylight will reveal all.

To work or not to work?

Many Christians think heaven will be boring because they have the idea that there will be no work to do. Heaven as one long worship session with periods of rest in between certainly would seem a little less than a rich experience from the viewpoint of a Christian earthling.

At the beginning of time in the perfect plan of creation, God included fulfilling and satisfying work for Adam and Eve. They were placed in a garden to work it and take care of it. Now I have to confess that I am not an avid gardener but since I believe the Bible I have to officially record that looking after one must be a very happy experience because that's what God gave the first people to do. What is happy for me is that my wife loves tending our garden and all of our family are mightily happy with the flowers and plants that adorn our home and the vegetables and fruit which she grows to supply our dinner table.

Sadly, gardening became less enjoyable after the Fall. This isn't my excuse for not taking part, but if you know Genesis 3 you will recall that God put a curse on the ground and told Adam that from now on work would be painful toil and 'by the sweat of your brow you will eat your food'. The message is clear. Work has changed from being a fun, creative activity to a tough means of earning a living.

So what about the new heavens and new earth? Will there be work to do or will it be one long eternal holiday? I think many of us who have the privilege of enjoying holidays would say that we are very grateful for them. Whether you stretch out on a sun-soaked white beach on the Mediterranean doing very little or stomp across the hills of England's Lake District, it is a rest. But I bet that many of us would not vote to stay on holiday for ever and ever. We want the challenge of something to get our teeth into. We want the satisfaction of ending a day and feeling we've done something worthwhile. We were not made for lives of leisure, but rather for using whatever gifts God has given us in serving him through serving other people.

If we are getting back to the Garden of Eden, to creation as God originally intended it, then there will certainly be work to do in the new heavens and new earth. But it will not be drudgery. There will not be stress attached to it. Instead, there will be the deep satisfaction of the kind that God experienced when he had worked for six days, designing and creating the universe; the same kind of fulfilment he gave to Adam and Eve in Eden.

All creatures great and small

I was roused from my bed this morning by a snuffling noise, directed at the crack under our bedroom door. There was a snuffle, a snort and then a whine or two. It happens on many mornings. We open the door and the bedroom is full of dogs. With their tails wagging so hard you would think it would hurt, they parade round the bedroom with squeals of delight to greet us for the new day. If, like me, you are a nature lover and especially if you have pets, you can't help wondering if there will be animals in heaven. It's the first question a lot of people have asked me when they discover I am writing a book about heaven.

One thing is for sure, the whole living world of nature is not here by accident, because God cares deeply about it. Jesus made a very direct statement to this effect. 'Look at the birds of the air; they do not sow or reap or store away in barns, and yet your heavenly father feeds them' (Matt. 6:26). He goes on to say that we are more valuable to God than birds. But this doesn't negate the obvious message that God cares enough about our feathered friends to see that they have food.

I find it very hard to think that God would go to such extraordinary lengths now if he does not have any future plans for all the intricately made creatures that he has designed. The incredible variety of creatures, and their extraordinary designs which enable them to live in their various habitats is staggering. The pleasure we gain from their colours, shapes and in some cases, antics, all point to an immense effort put in by the Creator. Could God abandon the entire animal kingdom as being a temporary thing designed only for this era? Something tells me not. David Lawrence makes the shrewd observation: 'An earth without animals would be a completely different sort of

132

earth, not a renewed version of this one.' If the new heavens and new earth are going to be the kind of environment we will recognise and appreciate, and contain the best of all that we have previously known, it certainly makes sense to me that there will be animals there.

That is, of course, a different thing from saying that the particular animals that have been special to us on this earth will be resurrected. David Lawrence again:

> Since the Bible does not indicate that animals have an eternal spirit within them, and they do not feature in biblical glimpses into the spiritual heavenly 'waiting room' of Paradise, it is perhaps safer to picture a huge new act of creation in which another animal kingdom is brought into being, an animal kingdom which will look like this one but is not this one resurrected.

So I'm looking forward to some animals to enjoy in heaven, but I'm not sure that the snuffles under my bedroom door will be from the same border terrier which woke me this morning.

Genesis 1 tells us that originally God made every living creature a herbivore. Isaiah 11 looks forward to the day when an incredible state of grace will be restored, and there will be an end to 'nature red in tooth and claw'. Imagine a field full of wolves, lambs, leopards, goats, calves, lions, cows and bears, and you've got the picture. And don't forget that 'a little child will lead them'. I think I'm going to look for a dandelion and find the biggest grizzly bear around, to see if he likes it.

We Christians have so much to look forward to! If we die in the normal way, our spirits will fly into the presence of the One we have always longed to be with, along with all those others who have left and gone ahead of us. Then on that 'day' we can look forward to a whole new phase of life. Our resurrection bodies will be whole and strong. The new heavens and new earth will suddenly be all around us, cleansed, pure, shining bright.

Anticipating all this just around the corner is delicious – but what difference does it make to life now? I find it affects almost everything! Let me explain.

Part Three

Living in the Light of Heaven

10

Eternal Instincts

I can truthfully say that hardly a day passes without my thinking of heaven. This present life is sometimes such a tough and painful thing that I constantly remind myself of what is to come. It isn't simply an escape mechanism. Reviewing where I'm heading helps maintain a healthy perspective on life. The devil and his committees below constantly work on new schemes. A favourite line of attack is to induce amnesia in their target: forgetfulness of God's past faithfulness, present generosity and future promises. But Satan has a big barrier to overcome, for God 'has set eternity in the hearts' of us all (Eccles. 3:11). Deep inside you and me is a longing for something lasting, good, right . . . to fill an emptiness within: an instinctive, God-given, eternity-shaped vacuum.

The eternal value of love

Most of us at some time in life have experiences which seem almost to be hints of eternity. Experiences of love – genuine, caring, unselfish – would have to be high on any list. Romantic love is certainly on a high plane – the New Testament likens the relationship between Christ and his Church to a bridegroom and bride. Perhaps it is the eternal value of love that makes all of us want to be loved. An unloved child is less likely to thrive, and there is deep pain when a loving relationship is lost by death, divorce or whatever.

Love stories will sell books and films until the end of time. You would think there have been so many love stories written that we would get bored with them! But no, the theme chimes with something deep inside us, and we will never tire of stories of real love. True stories fascinate us all the more. Perhaps they give us hope that all that we deeply wish for could come true. Sue and I have our own love story (which you can read in *Heaven on Your Doorstep*, Hodder, 1986). We have had our ups and downs like every other couple, but now and again I have been intrigued to see people fascinated by our happiness. Since we are pretty much incompatible, the whole thing is a great advertisement for what God can do.

Not so long ago we celebrated our twenty-fifth wedding anniversary, during a speaking tour in Australia. By the kindness of a generous friend, part of the celebration was a week's holiday on Hinchinbrook Island, a hideaway off the coast of Queensland. It has 40,000 acres of sub-tropical forest with shady walks cut through it. There are seven white sandy beaches, but to keep the environment unspoiled and the wildlife protected, only forty people are allowed to stay on the island at any one time. It was like a little piece of paradise and we could never have chosen a better place for a second honeymoon.

We stayed in a sort of tree house only a few yards back from the beach, and looking out over the gentle curve of Orchard Bay. Each day we swam in the warm clear waters of the bay, and paddled in a canoe around rocky promontories. It didn't feel too much different from being like Adam and Eve in the Garden of Eden. We hardly saw anyone else during the daytime, but each evening everyone congregated in the dining room for dinner. There were several other couples, some married, some not. It seemed to us that some of them were snatching what they hoped might be a little chunk of happiness, albeit illicit, in an otherwise unhappy and lonely life.

I chose one evening to give Sue a surprise. I asked the chef to bake a twenty-fifth wedding anniversary cake. Sue was duly amazed as the waitress put the gorgeous cake down on our table. We then took the rest of the cake round to offer to all the other guests at their tables. As each one congratulated us on the anniversary, I could read a great deal of incredulity in some faces: 'How come these two have managed twenty-five years?'

'You two are so lucky,' breathed one lady.

'Please excuse me disagreeing with you,' I said as gently as I could, scooping cake on to her plate. 'But it's really not luck that we thank, but the wonderful God we have.' I smiled my best smile and we moved on to the next table. Her eyes had shown that she had glimpsed a hint of something eternal and desperately wanted it. The next day she came to our room and we talked. She had been married twice and was living with a third man. We did our best to share the much more important love which her Creator had for her. As we waved her goodbye on the jetty at the end of our holiday, we prayed that God would press home that eternal instinct.

Life and love focused on heaven

Eternal love is something we long for and will know in heaven. God knows that for most of us that kind of feeling is rather unreal at times. Have you found that God has very generously given you one or two experiences that opened your eyes a little? Perhaps something that focused your life more on eternity and heaven?'

One of the greatest love stories of this century, for me, is that of Sheldon and Davy Vanauken. It is all the more extraordinary because their very special love relationship underwent a transition, through the influence of C. S. Lewis, to become a Christ-centred marriage. Long before they knew Christ, however, they had made a pact which bound them together in a depth few couples probably ever experience. The story is told in the autobiography of their love by Sheldon, entitled *A Severe Mercy*.

Worshipping their relationship almost like a religion, they bound themselves to have no secrets from one another and formulated a structure to keep outside influences from spoiling their relationship – they called it 'the Shining Barrier'. They even went so far as deciding against having children, lest they should spoil the magic of their being together, and they pledged that if one should die, the other partner should take their own life in an attempt to follow them, wherever they might be.

One of their dreams had been to buy a boat and go exploring. Their dream came true with a schooner named *Grey Goose*. Spending time exploring the islands and ports of the east coast of the USA around Chesapeake Bay, they had a new dimension added to their lives after a hot summer day with a fine fresh breeze to sail on. After a flaming sunset they turned into their bunks to sleep. Sheldon takes up the story:

Some time in the night I awoke, feeling the yacht swinging at her anchor. A stream of lovely cool air was pouring down the forward hatch. I got up soundlessly and emerged from the hatch as far as my waist. At the same instant Davy popped out of the after hatch and crept forward along the deck to where I stood, half out of the hatch. The breeze had sprung up and backed to north so that it was coming straight in the mouth of the cove, though not strongly enough to cause any worry about the anchor holding. It had blown every bit of humidity and sultriness away. The air was cool and fresh. Ten thousand brilliant stars arched across the sky. But what transfixed us was phosphorescence. Every little wave rolling into the cove was crested with cold fire. The anchor rode on a line of fire going down into the depths, and fish moving about left trails of fire. The night of the sea-fire. Davy had crept near to me, still crouching, and I put my arm around her, and she snuggled close.

Neither of us spoke, not so much as a whispered word. We were together, we were close, we were overwhelmed by a great beauty. I know that it seemed to us both that we were completely one: we had no need to speak. We remained so in timeless loveliness – was it hours? We never knew. All about us was the extraordinary beauty of the sea-fire and the glittering stars overhead. We were full of wonder – and joy. *Grey Goose* was alive, lifting to the little waves, and the tall dark masts were pencilling across the stars. The moment was utterly timeless; we didn't know that time existed; and it contained, therefore, some foretaste, it may be, of eternity. At last, still with no word spoken, we went below again and, in comfort and a great peace, slept.

Next day we did not know at all whether that timeless moment – that moment made eternity – had been hours long or minutes long. (*A Severe Mercy*, Hodder, 1977)

The extraordinary experience happened during their last few days living in the USA before they left to study at Oxford University. Sheldon describes it as an experience to prepare them for what they describe as their 'encounter with Light'. They were given this hint of eternity before they really believed, and some very special glimpses of that wider and bigger goal which their relationship would eventually become committed to following.

Heavenly happiness

Perhaps the biggest feature of eternal life in heaven is that we shall be happy.

So much of what we hope will bring happiness on earth does not deliver what we had imagined. Even the best things we pursue are never totally fulfilling. C. S. Lewis, in a sermon entitled 'The Weight of Glory' (8 June 1941), speaks of 'our desire which no natural happiness will satisfy'. Even the best relationships and happiness are merely 'hints and symbols' of what we will enjoy in heaven, and sadness and disappointment always accompany them. The shadow of total happiness always turns the corner 'a pace or two ahead of us'.

Lewis concludes that if nothing in this world can fully satisfy our desires now we can logically conclude that we were made for another world. We were, and we shall be there one day. And we shall be happy.

Of course it's true that unbelievers – or people from any religion, for that matter – can experience some degree of happiness they feel. But for Christians it has a rather special meaning. Jesus told us that to be truly 'happy' is a distinctive quality that belongs to the kingdom of heaven. He outlines this happiness in the Beatitudes (Matt. 5). Where the NIV and other translations use the word 'blessed', the Jerusalem Bible translates this as 'happy'. The Greek word *makarios* simply means 'happy'. In the Beatitudes Jesus shows the difference between most people's idea of being 'happy' and 'true happiness'. Jesus lists those who can be included in the category of having the real thing. At first sight, it is an odd list!

The poor in spirit
Those who mourn
The meek
Those who hunger and thirst for righteousness
The merciful
The pure in heart
The peacemakers
The persecuted

Quite a surprise selection! Not what you would get if you went out in the street and did an opinion poll asking the question, 'What categories of people would you describe as being happy?' You would get a rather different list.

Couples who are in love
The rich who have no money worries
The holidaymaker staying in a luxury resort
The man in the pub who has had a few drinks
The syndicate who won more than £10 million on the lottery last week
Etc., etc.!

As usual, Jesus gives the lie to notions that prevail in the world. To paraphrase the Beatitudes:

You might think rich people are happy – in fact those who consider themselves poor are truly happy.

You may think people who have never experienced bereavement or sorrow are happy – actually if you have been through an experience of suffering and known God's help, that is real happiness.

It looks as if leaders in society and influential people have the potential for happiness – but in fact if you are a meek person you will be happy.

You may think that people who do whatever they feel like and are not troubled by their consciences would be happy – that's not true and you will be happy if your main priority is to be at peace with your conscience and live a right life.

Powerful people who can impose their will to get what they want should be happy – but in fact they are not and the secret of happiness is to be a thoughtful person, merciful to others and considerate of what they want.

Anyone who achieves the ambitions of their heart and sees their dreams come true must be happy – that's not really so but if you have a pure heart you will be happy for you will see God.

You would think that a self-made, man who has negotiated hard to get what he wants and overpower his opponents must be satisfied and happy – no! Winning arguments by force doesn't make anyone happy, but making peace between people does, and you will then be not self-made, but someone whose life success is made by God.

You think you would be happy if you had no enemies and had a knack of coming to a compromise with people who see things differently from you – no, you will actually be happy if you pursue what you know to be right, even if it means other people persecute you.

No wonder Jesus upset people. He challenges every assumption of the worldly person in every different area of life and especially about the secret of happiness. These perspectives of being happy – through humbly knowing God, being at peace with him and with others, living in a way that is pleasing to him, living in truth – are true in spite of physical circumstances. This is how Christ lived, in the knowledge of his Father's will and purpose, and this is how we can live, having faith in the Father's will.

Our lifelong ambition to be like Jesus and be close to him will be fulfilled in heaven. We shall be with him every moment of eternity. We shall be completely absorbed in fulfilling his purposes for us in the kingdom of heaven. That will be true happiness indeed. Heading towards that will deeply affect our attitudes and lifestyle while we're still on planet earth.

11

When the Going Gets Tough

Despite the happiness we can look forward to in heaven, it still rings true that varying kinds of deep pain are part of life here on earth. Humanly speaking there is very little comfort to be found. However, we are offered the promise of resources from God's grace. And to give us hope when we feel hopeless, we are reminded of all that lies ahead, regardless of our present situation.

On his third missionary journey, in the early spring of AD 57, Paul sat down at his desk in Corinth and wrote to Christians in Rome: 'I consider that our present sufferings are not worth comparing with the glory that will be revealed in us.' Paul had the authority to say that. Like his master, he continually travelled and had no proper home, no security, money or possessions to speak of. He had suffered physical danger and violence. But because he had this life in perspective with the next, he kept his eye on his destination

Hope comes from looking ahead. Vision and optimism come from living one day at a time, looking at what God has promised for the present and the future. You may not be like me, but I frequently wake early in the morning with a lurking sense of foreboding. Problems, worries and fears seem to have a habit of knocking on

146

the door to my mind at an early hour. Things get off to a very depressing start if I open the door and have a good look at them. Paul obviously did a 'present' and 'future' comparison before he got out of bed each day. Every Christian taking a check on 'present sufferings' and 'future glory' is bound to have a better chance of a good day. Hope is a huge thing that can outweigh all manner of suffering experiences, however heavy they may seem.

This is even true of the earth around us. We are bombarded with bad news about the health of planet earth and feel pain and depression. Long before you or I knew the words pollution, acid rain or Chernobyl, Paul expressed exactly the same hurt at the suffering of God's beautiful planet. He wrote: 'The creation waits in eager expectation . . . in hope that [it] will be liberated from its bondage to decay and brought into . . . glorious freedom' (Rom. 8:19–21). So every time I see a news item about the inevitable running down of the environment I remind myself: there is hope. The foreboding feeling that could spoil a glorious country view or stop a smile rising as I watch a dozen delicate white butterflies dancing on the heather bush in our garden is diffused. I remind myself: it is not the inevitable end. The whole creation will be redeemed, renewed. We have every reason to look up with a smile, not down with a frown. The Garden of Eden is coming back.

When we fail

Living with heaven in view also does glorious things for the way in which you see yourself. Growing up in England, I was totally ignorant of a rather important fact. It was actually not until I first visited the USA that I discovered I had a 'self-image'. In the efficient way that our American cousins have of classifying things, I discovered that the way I view myself, in various aspects of my life, can be described as 'high' or 'low'.

I had a real problem with this. There were times when I was very fed up with my lack of consideration for other people, constant tripping up over the same temptations, and had a general depressed feeling with living in this flesh. In fact, quite definitely a 'low self-image' in this respect.

But then at other times I rejoiced in having the Holy Spirit living within me. I knew myself to be redeemed, forgiven and on my way to heaven. I knew I possessed a new nature, I was born again, and that sin now had no power over me. My! All that lot made me feel better. Definitely 'high self-image'.

So now I had a problem. Which am I? High or low? Or am I some kind of nut, completely mixed up about my identity? I forgot to ask my American friends all about this before I came back to England so I was left with the ongoing dilemma. I discovered the answer, not by going back to America, but by asking St Paul. In Romans 7 he plunges into the depths of a hopeless despair about himself. He knows what is good but cannot do it. He knows what is bad but continually trips up. Feeling this terrible inner tension, he expresses just exactly what I feel on my 'low' days.

'What a wretched man I am! Who will rescue me from this body of death?' But then he heaves a great sigh of relief, because he knows where to look for hope. 'Thanks be to God – through Jesus Christ our Lord!' (Rom. 7:24, 25). Paul returns to this tension in Romans 8 and says we are a bit like the rest of creation, as we 'groan inwardly as we wait eagerly for our adoption, the redemption of our bodies' (verse 23).

So in a sense he doesn't resolve the tension. He admits his great weakness and the perfectly valid feelings of a low self-image in this area. But he is full of hope. Because of all that Christ has done; because of what will one day inevitably come to pass at the end of this era; and because of the process now going on within him, he is hopeful. The high self-image is there too. One day these weak bodies that have caused us so much heartache will be redeemed, exchanged for a resurrection body, and so our adoption will be complete. We shall come into our inheritance as children of God and we shall be whole.

This is a wonderful antidote for the kind of depressive feelings of low self-image we all experience. Paul knew all about this because he says: 'in this hope we were saved . . . if we hope for what we do not yet have, we wait for it patiently' (Rom. 8:24, 25). So in my lows I look up at the highs and remind myself that that is where it's all going to end up. Heaven brings hope. What a relief! I shall not be stuck in this frail failing selfish shell for much longer. Great!

Actually Romans shows us Christians that we are between two stages. It reassures us that 'we are God's children' (Rom. 8:16). Paul goes on to tell us that if that really is true then we are 'heirs of God and co-heirs with Christ.' That means we are going to inherit something. Verse 23 tells us that we have received the first down payment of our inheritance (the first fruits of the Spirit) but we also 'await eagerly for our adoption, the redemption of our bodies'. This is our coming of age and the full realisation of our inheritance in Christ: the final stage of our adoption at the resurrection.

And Paul gives us an extraordinary sense of oneness with Jesus when he describes us as 'co-heirs with Christ' (verse 17) and then says we are 'predestined to be conformed to the likeness of his Son, that he might be the firstborn among many brothers and sisters' (verse 29). Jesus has shared our experience of birth, life and death. He, our older brother, has gone before us in resurrection.

Helpful hurts

God obviously will use drastic methods to keep our eyes on eternal things. He is prepared to let us be hurt in order to help us. So that we don't waste our lives but live in the light of heaven, he may allow things we would never choose, to keep us on track. David certainly found this. 'Before I was afflicted I went astray but now I obey your word' (Ps. 119:67).

Whatever Paul's thorn in the flesh was, God certainly used it to keep his mind on the job. With all that he achieved, he could easily have become proud and boastful and thought himself to be in a different league, a kind of 'super-Christian'. But instead his circumstances caused him to feel weak and to realise that God's strength would show up best through his weakness. This seems surprising since Paul indicates that God allowed a messenger of Satan to torment him with a thorn after he had had amazing experiences of being transported into heavenly realms.

I bet you have longed for a deeper and closer experience of God. Perhaps at times you have pleaded with him to give you some special vision, ecstatic experience or some kind of touch on your life that would change you forever, transport you to heaven and cause you to be different for the rest of your life. I am not sure whether Paul asked for it, but he certainly got just that sort of treatment. I have heard a few people tell of visions and experiences, read numerous books with accounts of close encounters of a special kind with

God, but I don't think any of them come anything near 2 Corinthians 12.

Whatever it was Paul saw, felt and experienced that day, it was quite literally out of this world. So Paul finds himself tempted to boast rather than be humble (verse 7). He is tempted to think how special he must be to warrant this treatment, rather than how special God is to give such a generous dose of blessing. And then he realises he must boast not in himself but in God's power made perfect in our weakness – he even *delights* in his own weaknesses (verse 9).

We may be lifted to another plane not previously experienced. But so that our feet stay on planet earth and we don't think we have become angels; so that we realise how great God is rather than how great we have become; so that we live in the light of heaven, rather than thinking we have somehow made it there and everything is different now, God may well allow us to be brought down to earth with a bump. Heavenly experiences are often followed by thorns in the flesh. They keep us humble, help us realise that we're not so special. They also prevent us being so heavenly minded that we're no earthly use.

When the clouds loom

Do you ever find that a black cloud comes over you, full of all your present failings as well as your past sins? It seems particularly to afflict us when there's something to do for the Lord. Just when you want to feel on good form, brimming with godly bonhomie, that rotten old black cloud can appear. It gives you the feeling that you are completely inadequate to do anything for God. Even if other people have told you you've got certain gifts, you don't feel it can possibly be true. Or even if it is true and you have got the gifts, your mind and heart are full of something telling you that you are just not good enough to use those gifts for God. You keep on tripping up and falling flat and you've made such a mess of things in the past.

It is no wonder that the Bible calls Satan 'the accuser'. The entire contents of that black cloud is cunningly composed by committees that regularly meet down in hell. They pick on just the right ingredients to maximise the effect they want to achieve. The good news is that they are just like any cloud you see in the sky. Clouds can look so solid – in a clear blue sky you can almost mistake a bank of white clouds for a mountain range. But even a small puff of wind will blow them away. These black clouds can seem immovable unless you know the secret of how to shift them. The most effective gust of wind to blow them away comes from a good grasp of God's forgiveness through Christ and knowing that from the moment he enters your life, a process begins, transforming you day by day into the person he wants you to be.

When death prevails

Perhaps the biggest area in which living in the light of heaven answers our needs is how we face the loss of someone we love. Times of illness, narrow escapes from accidents, old age and a host of other things constantly remind us that life is not forever and that death is final. We may experience the agony of parting, perhaps without the opportunity of saying goodbye – the finality of a closed door which we know cannot be opened.

Any such circumstances can overwhelm us with a sense of despair. A dark cloud can descend. Without a faith, a belief in life after death, we can sink into despair. But best of all for a Christian is the promise of reunion with those we love.

Some years ago various things needed mending in our home and we called in Ted Weaver, a local man who could 'fix anything'. Over the next few years he fixed just about everything in our house from blocked drains to missing roof tiles, from dripping taps to problem chimneys. He was not only a hard worker, but also excellent company. Then one day he wasn't so well. Eventually after tests the news came through – Ted had cancer. Then he had a stroke. Ted lost his speech and was paralysed. When I visited him it really sank in. His frightened eyes and now feeble body stirred something deep inside me. It was not possible to talk but I stayed with him a while, talked briefly with his wife Ruth and then drove home. As I drove I hammered the steering-wheel with fury. 'Life was never meant to be like this,' I raged. Ted died a few days later.

Ted Weaver was the first person with whom I have ever been through the process of friendship, illness, dying and death. I did not find it easy to conduct his thanksgiving service. But it was made easier by an illustration which I believe God gave me. It was early May and on a country walk I suddenly came across a baby chestnut tree. It was only about nine inches tall, but it seemed to be bursting with spring life as it struggled upwards. I looked at the thick trunk of the chestnut tree standing a few feet away, towering above me and spreading its majestic branches and foliage. The little tree seemed to whisper, 'I'll be up there as big and beautiful as that soon.' It was a picture of the brave new life, unafraid and ready to go. I knelt down beside it and then I saw its former life. Only just under the soil and partially visible was the unattractive remains of what had once been a conker. I scratched a little more and then gently held in my hand a cluster of earth containing the old dying remains and the start of a new life. It was exactly what I wanted Ted's family to know.

Of course that does not mean there is no grief. In so many ways Christians are just as vulnerable and have just the same pain thresholds as everyone else. The difference is that we have a perspective on life that can accommodate death. We have resources to draw on because God promises us his grace to cope and we have the power of his indwelling Holy Spirit. The thing that keeps us from total despair is that we know there is a future. We have a hope.

Living in the light of heaven makes the most incredible difference in this arena. As usual Paul understands that Christians can have feelings of despair and hopelessness. He writes:

> Brothers and sisters, we do not want you to be ignorant about those who fall asleep, or to grieve like the rest, who have no hope. We believe that Jesus died and rose again and so we believe that God will bring with Jesus those who have fallen asleep in him. (1 Thess. 4:13)

We shall certainly grieve, but it will be a different experience because we know a secret. Jesus is coming back and will bring with him those who have gone ahead of us. Paul sketches in a few more details.

> For the Lord himself will come down from heaven, with a loud command, with the voice of the archangel and with the trumpet call of God, and the dead

in Christ will arise first. After that, we who are still alive and are left will be caught up together with them in the clouds to meet the Lord in the air. And so we will be with the Lord forever. Therefore encourage each other with these words. (1 Thess. 4:16–18)

It is only a matter of time until this great reunion party. If grief is a daily factor in your life, read 1 Thessalonians 4 regularly and ask God to plant this picture firmly in your heart. If he does that for us, we shall not grieve like others who have no hope.

If you are someone who has lost a child, husband or wife, you might feel that what I have written may be not what you have experienced. It may even sound rather harsh. I suppose that the whole of our Christian experience is a process of entering into the blessings of the promises of God by faith. I don't think those things usually happen in an instant. In many areas of life it is a process. Having friends who have experienced overwhelming grief followed by overwhelming hope has been a real encouragement to me.

Sue's mother went to be with her Lord some three years ago now, after a long period of ill health. She was the sweetest person you could wish to meet, gentle, unthreatening, always concerned for other people, with a love for her peaceful garden. Losing her was obviously an incalculable loss. However, believing that release from ill health was a blessing for her gave us a sense of gratitude to God for a wonderful life, rather than despairing grief. Living in the light of heaven made the most profound practical difference as we settled down to life again, without Granny living next door.

Loss differs in intensity. Of course I recognise that

losing an older loved one, who has had their life, is very different from losing a child with the added pain of all the expectations that will now be unfulfilled.

Nigel and Helen Cooke started their family and had three lovely girls. They longed for a boy and during the years that followed Helen first gave birth to twin boys and later to another boy. The tough thing was that they lost all three sons. Their dreams were dashed. Sitting by our fireside chatting over their feelings, I was really quite surprised to discover how they reacted. Helen remembered the last boy, Duncan, best.

'I was enjoying feeding him, cuddling him and revelling in having a boy. But it wasn't long before he developed breathing difficulties and they took him into intensive care. A week later he died.'

The fire flickered in the quietness and I asked gently, 'Were you angry with God?'

'No. I was at peace that God was in control. I knew the hospital had done everything. I never prayed that he would live. I never fought with God about it.'

'But you must have grieved?'

'Oh yes. I remember crying but I knew my boy was in heaven. I told a nurse that the child was given us by God and was in his hands. Yes, I grieved but we don't need to grieve like people "who have no hope", do we?'

Private grief is one thing. Celebrities who live life with the world looking on have even more to contend with. Roy Castle died at 5.15 a.m. on 2 September, 1994. Every newspaper headlined the story. It was not simply the passing of a much-loved all round entertainer at the age of 62, but also that he had battled with cancer for several years. The media were largely preoccupied with the reaction of his widow, Fiona: 'No flowers, no fuss, no mourning – just lots of joy.'

This is what she said and every newspaper reported it. It was stunningly different news. Good news. 'I am OK, I am fine', said Fiona. 'There has been a lot of laughter, there have been tears, and we have all prayed together. We have such a strong faith and we know that he has gone to be with Jesus – he has been given eternal life.'

The *Daily Mail* editorial commented, 'Few could have faced the end with more grace and more courage. Few could have turned a death sentence into such a triumphant affirmation of life.'

That's what I call living in the light of heaven.

12

A Certain Future

It is a wonderful thing to know who you are. If you have ever found yourself in a situation where you feel you don't fit, you will know what I mean. When you go to a party, and find to your horror that you don't know a soul, your confidence can take a knock and you think 'Help! What am I doing here?' Or maybe there is a meeting, function or activity with a group of people you know and with whom you sometimes play an organisational part. But on this occasion it's not clear who is doing what. You have a slightly muddly feeling as the thing goes on, wondering whether you ought to be stepping out to the front or whether someone else will do it. No one has quite spelled out your status in this particular situation so you're not sure of your identity.

Living in the light of heaven can give us a new sense of identity and confidence. We sometimes meet people with a seemingly unshakable sense of spiritual authority, power and vision, and we secretly wonder, 'How come they are like that and I am so much less certain?' You wonder if they were just born like it. Or have they had experiences with God which made them like it? Or has the school of life taught them lessons we haven't yet learned?

Paul possessed the most extraordinary energy and sense

of call. If I ever become 10 per cent of the Christian he was, or achieve 1 per cent of the ministry workload he cheerfully carried, I shall be more than happy. What was his secret? For a long time I rather crossly told the Lord that I thought it was pretty unfair he had made me, me and Paul, Paul. I unsubtly hinted to the Lord that if only he had given me a good few spoonfuls more call, energy and vision in my chromosomes, the kingdom of God might be galloping ahead like it did in the first century. My Christian life would be more abundant and my ministry more fruitful. The Lord was very patient with me and I finally realised it wasn't just Paul's genes. It was his appreciation of what God has done for every Christian, of what is happening right now in heavenly realms. He was living each day in the light of heaven.

A sense of purpose

Paul's sense of identity and purpose is evident in his letter to Christians living in Ephesus. In prison in Rome around AD 60, Paul doesn't simply sit there waiting for time to pass. He lets his faith soar to places you and I have probably never been. He shares his discoveries and blesses the Christians at Ephesus and the rest of us down the centuries who have read that same letter ever since.

Being in prison would upset and disorientate most of us. I have visited a number of prisons. Each time it has been to encourage someone I knew, to preach the gospel and to share God's Word. Each time I have known that before long I will be walking out again, a free man. It is a very different thing to know that you are not free to walk out.

People in prison tell me that all the achievements of their life fall away. You may have had a happy home, a successful career or a good job, been a respected member of your community. The security and confidence that these roles and achievements would normally give are stripped away in prison. Paul was no exception. His status as an apostle and church leader, his reputation as a preacher and church planter – all these things were not so real and buoyant now.

His conditions were probably more like an 'open prison' because he lived in a rented house and was allowed visitors (Acts 28:30). But when he wrote to the Ephesian Christians he was still to be under house arrest for another two or three years (and he had no idea at that time he would ever be released). He was probably only free for a few years and then back in jail around AD 66. That time it was a cold dungeon and he was chained like a common criminal. His second letter to Timothy gives us some details.

How do you think you'd get on in prison? Do you have a sense of self-identity and confidence in your status with God that would make a dynamic difference in a test like that? Paul certainly did. Ephesians tells us some of the secrets.

The secret of confidence

The first secret is praising God. Yes, sitting in Rome, in prison, under house arrest, Paul is praising God. Whatever for? Because He is 'the God and Father of our Lord Jesus Christ, who has blessed us in the heavenly realms with every spiritual blessing in Christ' (Eph. 1:3). Paul rises above his circumstances to burst out in praise to God because his heart is full of the wonder that every Christian is united with the exalted Christ and has already received 'every spiritual blessing' that can be enjoyed in and poured out from heavenly realms.

160

Do you often pray, 'Lord bless me'? Paul praised God for already giving him every possible blessing he could ever think of. He obviously realised that God has already poured out every kind of blessing from heaven. It is now our privilege to reach out and take what is available. Instead of battering the gates of heaven, pleading with God, Paul is praising God for blessings there on tap. We only have to reach out our empty cup and fill it.

In today's world, I can't think of many illustrations of good things provided on tap free for anyone who will take them. But only yesterday I stumbled on just such a thing. I am actually writing this part of the book staying in the lovely Swiss village of Wengen, leading a Christian holiday party. The majestic snow-capped peaks of the Eiger, Monch and Jungfrau tower above the village. Endless footpaths wind through the forests and mountain pastures. Yesterday the sun blazed down out of a cloudless blue sky and I stopped on the pathway beside a fountain of blessing. Some kind Swiss farmer had tapped a mountain spring so that it poured out of a pipe into a wooden trough hollowed out of a fir-tree trunk. Beside the footpath, weary walkers like me could stop, hold out empty cupped hands and find them filled from an endless rich refreshing supply.

Paul gives a refreshing list of blessings from heavenly realms provided on tap to give us a true sense of our identity and status. Here are some of the things God has already done for you.

He chose you.
He made a plan for you to be set apart for him.
He has forgiven you.
He adopted you for his son or daughter.
He has lavished the riches of God's grace on you.

He has given you the Holy Spirit, a deposit guaranteeing your inheritance.

He has given you all wisdom and understanding through the Holy Spirit.

He has let you in on the secret mystery of his will.

All that comes from having a little peep into 'the heavenly realms'; from realising what a difference the past and present activities of heaven make to our lives; from living in the light of heaven. Now you might think that one glimpse into the heavenly realms tells us enough of Paul's secret but we would be wrong. Glimpses into the 'heavenly realms' pop up five times in Ephesians.

A foot on either side

Heaven was never far from Paul's thinking. In fact in a very real way I think you could say that Paul lived and breathed heaven, because in one sense he knows that every Christian is already there. No, I know that we are still living on earth. But Paul wants us to get thoroughly into the way of thinking that all of us already have a great big stake in heaven now.

To hasten our soul's ascent in this direction, Paul prays for his readers:

That the eyes of their hearts may be enlightened.

To know the hope to which God has called them.

To experience the riches of God's glorious inheritance.

To know God's incomparably great power.

And now Paul is aching to get to his punchline to say how this involves us: 'And God raised us up with Christ and seated us with him in the heavenly realms' (Eph. 2:6). We are already there! We are seated with Christ in heaven right now even though our feet are still touching planet earth. Isn't that why we sometimes feel, 'Stop the world – I want to get off!'? Isn't that why occasionally we have a deep ache that tells us, 'this world is not my home'? We already have a home in heaven. We are already taking our reserved seats in heavenly realms.

When you know this for sure, actually stepping over to the other side to take your seat is made so much easier. Herman Lunger, a young German, was executed by the Nazis during World War II. The night before he died this is what he wrote to his parents:

When this letter comes to your hands I shall no longer be among the living . . . If you ask what state I am in I can only answer I'm in a joyous mood and filled with great anticipation, for this day brings the greatest hour of my life. For me believing is going to be seeing, hope will become possession and I shall for ever share in Him who is mine. Today is the great day on which I return to my Father. How can I fail to be excited and full of joy.

Until we meet in the presence of Christ,

Your joyful Herman

(Herman Lunger, *Dying We Live*, Fontana, 1958)

Herman has now taken his seat. While we wait for our turn, God is still going to be doing more for us. In the coming ages he will show 'the incomparable riches of his grace' (Eph. 2:7). And God has worked on us to get us to this point, not just to sit back in luxury and enjoy all his blessings but 'to do good works which God prepared in advance for us to do' (Eph. 2:10). Living in the light of heaven means that we know the extraordinary security of having one foot in the grave – well, one foot in heaven! But the other foot is firmly planted on earth, where God has important role for you and me. There are good things to do.

As we serve God, in fellowship with his people in the Church, two things happen. One is that 'the unsearchable riches of Christ' are unfolded to people around us who previously knew nothing about this glorious side of life (Eph. 3: 8, 9). God's second intention is that 'through the church, the manifold wisdom of God should be made known to the rulers and authorities in the heavenly realms' (Eph. 3:10). God's power at work through you and me is a witness to angels and demons, to those with any kind of role to play in the heavenlies.

Knowing your enemy

Finally, Paul knows the realities he is facing in the spiritual realms. It is not his circumstances, feelings or hostile people he is fighting. He knows exactly where to place the blame, and concentrate his struggle: 'Take your stand against the devil's schemes. For our struggle is not against flesh and blood, but against the rulers, against the authorities, against the powers of this dark world and against the spiritual forces of evil in the heavenly realms' (Eph. 6:11, 12).

Living in the light of heaven isn't all roses. But Paul urges us on to tower above our circumstances and realise who is our real enemy. When you have the light of heaven on your pathway, you don't waste effort on the symptoms – you can deal directly with the cause.

A Certain Future

Some years ago an ordinary schoolteacher and house-wife became burdened with the sliding standards of broadcasting in the UK. Not just rubbish, but things that a Christian could only describe as evil were pouring out of our television screens day after day. Mary Whitehouse felt called by God to do something. She founded the National Viewers and Listeners Association and went into battle to campaign for cleaner television. If you want to become a rich popular national hero and superstar, this is not a good move. The personal abuse and ridicule didn't take long to gather momentum. It would not be an exaggeration to say that Mary was publicly crucified over many years for her activities.

She stayed in our home some years after starting on the campaign trail. Sitting at breakfast one morning, I asked her how she coped with the volume of hurt which would have sunk many of us without trace. She didn't reply for a few seconds, but then looked up with her bright blue eyes.

'Yes, at first it was very hurtful and I didn't think I could go on. Then I realised that all this abuse wasn't really directed at me – it was the forces of evil making a comeback at the goodness of God.' She smiled and then revealed her secret. 'After that it was easier. Every time something came flying my way I reached out before it hit me and threw it up to the Lord.' She looked up at the ceiling and made a gesture with her hands as if hurling a football skywards. 'This one is yours, Lord. You can deal with this a lot better than I can.'

Living in the light of heaven enables you and me to identify the source of things that hurt us and makes dealing with them less difficult. A glimpse into the heavenly realms not only helps us lift our hearts in praise but also helps us to cope in dealing with darkness.

13

Coming Soon

When my brother and I were small boys living in a rambling farmhouse in Sussex, future events – especially Christmas – certainly made a huge difference to our daily life. As the excitement built up, we became less and less controllable. The days before Christmas were filled with sessions of making little presents. I can remember Mum whispering that what Dad wanted most was some Smarties and that if I put them in a matchbox that would be a nice surprise for him because he wouldn't be expecting it when he took the wrapping off. My visit to the village shop to procure the Smarties was cloaked in secrecy and the delight of springing a surprise. The bell on the door always jangled welcome as you walked into 'Aldridge's Stores'. And behind the battered counter was the round dumpy figure of Mrs Aldridge herself – equally welcoming. I whispered in her ear. 'I want a small packet of Smarties but Daddy mustn't know. I can't tell you why 'cos it's a secret.' Mrs Aldridge gave me a knowing nod and reached for the clandestine item. She put it in a plain brown paper bag and I rushed out of the shop.

Unseen preparations were being made for the big day, but we were never allowed to see even the slightest trace of them. The suspense was unbearable. We lay in bed each night hearing the occasional noise downstairs and trying to interpret it. Parental injunctions that 'it really is high time you were asleep now' seemed intolerable. After many Christmases of sleeplessness, my mother decided that we would adopt the Scandinavian Christmas tradition of presents on Christmas Eve. This diffused a good deal of the anticipation in a pleasant sort of way and Christmas was much more peaceful after that.

But you get the idea. A great day was coming. We didn't just sit there apathetically waiting for it. It was the kind of *waiting in eager anticipation* which deeply affected us. There was also an awareness of unseen activities in preparation for the day. We knew things were going on even though we couldn't see them.

Something of this enthusiastic excitement is what we Christians feel as we anticipate heaven. Paul catches the excitement of what is coming soon in Romans 8:23. I was brought up on the RSV translation, 'We wait for adoption as sons, the redemption of our bodies.' That version doesn't really express the anticipation packed into the Greek word Paul used for 'wait'. The NIV picks up the glint in Paul's eye and says 'we wait eagerly'.

If everything God promised us is really going to happen, we would be less than human if we didn't get a tiny bit excited. Children get excited over Christmas. A couple get excited looking forward to their wedding day. A businessman finds his heart pumping faster anticipating the benefits of a business deal. Living in the light of eternity just has to be a different experience from living expecting death to end it all.

Anne Benford is 91 years young and is my oldest prayer partner. She is still in church every Sunday and I have rarely seen her face wearing anything other than her usual beatific smile. I asked her recently, 'Are you looking forward to going to heaven, Anne?' She responded with a godly chuckly and simply said, 'I certainly am – I hope I'll be next!'

Life is not just what we see now, but what we know that God is preparing for us. Peter devotes the third chapter of his second letter entirely to the topic. The first part of the chapter tells us what is going to happen. The second part tells us what we ought to do about it. I don't think Peter had in mind a picture of a Christian sitting in an armchair watching television, wondering what time heaven would arrive. The looking forward he has in mind here is an *active* eager expectation (2 Peter 3:12–13).

A few weeks ago I was at Glasgow airport early in the morning waiting for a flight down to London. Due to an engine problem, it was delayed. As we passengers waited in the lounge at the departure gate, you could see people reacting in a variety of ways. A well-dressed executive paced up and down the length of the lounge, obviously worried he was going to miss an appointment. Another equally important-looking businessman tapped away on his laptop computer. Every eight minutes one agitated elderly lady went up to the desk and harassed the airline staff. Why were we late? Oh, yes, the broken engine. Why wasn't it ready yet? Well, she did hope everything would be mended soon because she was so looking forward to arriving at Heathrow and seeing her grandchildren. This was eager anticipation – but there was nothing active we could do to help things along.

However, there is something you and I can do to hasten the day that this era ends, and the new heavens and new earth begin. We can 'speed its coming', says Peter (verse 12). As we work to accomplish God's purposes, show his love, help others to repentance and faith, we are bringing the dawn of that great day nearer. What a thought!

Preparing for heaven

I can't remember many times in my life when someone has sat me down and given me a serious talking to about my life. Most of the time I have picked up the necessary information by a comment here or a hint there. But I do remember quite clearly a time when I was eighteen and about to go off to university and my Dad called me into his study for a serious talk. Yes, he had a good old-fashioned study and a sound old-fashioned approach to telling me what he thought I ought to know at this stage of my life. He pointed out that in a few weeks' time I would be away from home living on my own. So I needed to prepare myself to live a disciplined life, decide on a certain time to get up and a time to go to bed. I needed to decide to work hard because no one else was going to tell me to. I needed to make plans about how to budget my meagre financial resources. And he gave me some wise advice about girls and how to treat them with respect. He could see something important coming up and he wanted to point out to me what I ought to do about it.

Peter does exactly the same thing in his second letter. The end of an era is coming shortly and he wants us to know what we ought to be doing about it. Heaven is going to be here before we know it, so how does it affect us? The way Peter approaches it is to say everything is going to change shortly. Because of this fact, 'What kind of people ought you to be?' (2 Pet. 3:11). Peter knows that every meaningful scrap of theological information carries with it lifestyle imperatives. Knowledge about God and his ways (theology) is not designed just to interest us. It is intended to impact us, to change our lives. It has 'musts' and 'ought to' phrases attached to it. Peter continued, 'You ought to live holy and godly lives as you look forward to the day

169

of God' (vv.11–12). That may look like a short list with only short words in, but taking care of that could well keep us pretty busy for the rest of our lives.

The word 'holy' can have a rather old-fashioned dusty ring to it. It smells of musty monasteries, ancient dark churches and out-of-date hymn-books. In fact it doesn't mean any of those things. It literally means 'set apart' or 'different'. Glossy fashionable magazines usually contain at least one feature article on the life of a rich and famous superstar. We seem to be fascinated by people like this. They are different, set apart; some people dream of being like them. Our dream and privilege is to be different in another way. Surrounded by a world that is crooked and depraved, Paul says we 'shine like stars in the universe' (Phil. 2:15).

Being a godly person doesn't sound very cool, does it? But in actual fact what could be more exciting or worthwhile than wanting to become more like the God who made us? It stands out a mile that if you believe in God and you know him personally, you will want to be like him. I am regularly humbled by the knowledge that my faith is nothing more than an academic party piece unless belief in God leads me to be more godly; believing in the Holy Spirit makes me more holy; and believing in Jesus causes me to be more Christ-like.

'Since you are looking forward . . . make every effort to be found spotless, blameless and at peace with him' (2 Pet. 3:14). The standard of perfection Peter urges us towards is the same description he has given to Jesus, the Lamb of God, 'without blemish or defect' (1 Pet. 1:19). In a world where spots and blemishes are widely acceptable because 'nobody is perfect' and 'everyone has a weakness', Peter urges us to make a project of aiming at the perfection of Christ. You wouldn't think he would have needed to include an exhortation to be at peace with God when writing to Christians. But I think this down-to-earth, old, former fisherman is being realistic enough to recognise that while Christians do have peace with God as a result of being justified by faith, we can still displease him by failing to live in a way that pleases him. Pleasing ourselves doesn't require any effort at all – it comes quite naturally. Sacrificing our lives to serve others and to please God will require you and me to 'make every effort'.

Be on your guard

Peter is about to sign off but remembers three more things:

> Be on your guard.
> Grow in grace.
> Grow in the knowledge of Jesus Christ.

A faint smile always wants to surface on my face when someone earnestly tells me that they had a bit of trouble at their church . . . 'So some of us have started a new church and we are determined to run it along New Testament lines.' From the New Testament down to the present day there have been troubles in every local church. The New Testament church certainly had its fair share of fanatics who got carried away by some wrong doctrinal emphasis or power-hungry church leaders who took part of the flock away for their own reasons.

Peter knows about all this and leaves us with three powerful antidotes. If we are on guard for this kind of trouble in our fellowship, we won't be so likely to get carried away. If the gracious work is growing in us, this will be a good protection. (Would someone who knows us well say that you or I have 'grown in grace' over the past year?) And our knowledge of Jesus will keep us on track: both our personal daily relationship with him, and our wider knowledge of God and his ways and his Word. (Would people in your church describe you as someone who has this kind of knowledge?)

These instructions are developed in 1 Peter 4:7–11: 'The end of all things is near. Therefore be clear minded . . . self-controlled . . . pray.' Again, through growing in grace and knowing him and his purpose, we can achieve these things. 'Love each other deeply . . . offer hospitality . . . without grumbling.' This is how we work out fellowship that doesn't get distorted.

I may be wrong, but I sense that Peter writes with a certain desperation flowing through his pen. He feels the end is coming soon and there is so much to pay attention to if we are to hear Jesus's 'Well done!' Living in the light of heaven is a practical daily business. The urgency of the tasks still to be completed gives us a huge incentive to press on – more powerful than any business bonus-incentive scheme could ever be. The rewards are eternal.

And knowing that every day is numbered, Peter says, use whatever gift you have to serve others. Every act of service is some form of administering God's grace. When we are speaking, we should 'do it as one speaking the very words of God'. Forget the idea of scratching your head and trying to think of something to say for your sermon. Don't even count the cost of study and preparation. We haven't got long so give every talk as if it's your last. (Thank you, Peter – that bit is for me.)

He mentions also to anyone who serves that they should 'Do it with the strength God provides.' Isn't that obvious? Actually I don't think it is. There's all the difference in the world (and certainly in heaven) between serving whoever it may be (your family, your church, your employer, your customers) by working hard with the best you can give; or by doing what you do with a prayer breathed over it all, that God's touch may be there. God longs to infuse our efforts with his strength.

And don't forget who deserves the credit. I love it when someone praises me – and sometimes that is all right. But watch out; it's easy to steal what doesn't belong to you. Peter's aim is that 'in all things God may be praised'. Whether the same thing happens with you and me will depend on where we are setting our sights. I wish I had realised sooner just how important that can be.

14

Setting Our Sights on Heaven

Alongside our anticipation of heaven, the heavenly realities are nonetheless obscured by the distractions of daily life here on earth. We may reach the heights of Christian experience, but our spiritual perceptions are muzzy, and the sense of their reality is easily blotted out. Something whispers that we must have been dreaming on the days that we thought they were real.

I've just walked up from the Swiss village of Wengen to my favourite viewpoint, Hunnenfluh. The last time I walked this glorious little mountain path, the warm sunshine bathed the green alps and pine trees. The bright snow-capped mountains looked down on me from their majestic heights. Today the forest is shrouded in mist, the hills are cloud-covered and the snowy mountains completely invisible. All I can see is a murky glimpse through some trees into a fog. The whole atmosphere feels rather depressing. The appearance of sunny warmth and scenic mountain grandeur is banished into unreality. But even though I can't see them, I know that thousands of feet above me the mountain peaks are still there. I shall see them again when the clouds part and the sun shines through.

Living in the light of heaven involves constantly reminding yourself that heaven is real, never far away.

However invisible at any given moment, it is the one thing more real and inevitable than anything else you can think of. However permanent and secure other things sometimes feel or appear, nothing will ever prevent the glorious majesty of heaven bursting through the clouds into the full dawn of our experience one day.

A material world

Living in the light of heaven puts into perspective all those aspects which make up our daily lives: our homes, friends, holidays, hobbies, work. These are all part of the richness of life – but they are not its purpose. As we follow our 'dream purpose' with our sights on heaven, the 'parts' are kept in their place. The parts are not the dream. The person who has no dreams of heaven must find a dream to follow. There is no shortage of alternative dreams on offer: a special person, relationship or career; a lifestyle with dream homes, dream cars, dream holidays, dream leisure activities and possessions. They are the not-so-subtle hints that are intended to convey to others and bolster in us a sense of well-being and achievement. They are the 'little luxuries' which add that 'special touch' to life and make us feel important and significant. But they do not deliver all that they promise.

I pray frequently that my deepest dreams will be for projects with a value that far outlast the hollow and shortlived.

Make me Lord, a dreamer for your kingdom;
Plant in my heart heavenly desires,
Grant faith that can say, impossibilities shall be,
And vision lest a world should perish not knowing
    Thee.

Chris Bowater

Knowing full well exactly how we are made in our inner being, Jesus tells us where our hearts should be if they are to be satisfied. I can't believe he said it with a gentle, meek smile on his face, knowing how the seductive whisper of earthly things creeps into our souls and gains a firm foothold.

> Do not store up for yourselves treasures on earth, where moth and rust destroy, and where thieves break in and steal. But store up for yourselves treasures in heaven, where moth and rust do not destroy, and where thieves do not break in and steal. For where your treasure is, there your heart will be also. (Matt. 6:19–21)

Jesus obviously had in mind the kind of material trophies and trinkets we love to accumulate. Rust, decay, thieves and a hundred and one other things can either destroy their appeal or part us from them. Our hearts were never meant to be satisfied by these things. We need some possessions. We need clothes to wear. To make a home beautiful with attractive ornaments or works of art is not wrong. But what the Master warns us is that if our hearts are locked up in these treasures we will be unsatisfied. Then if we lose them in whatever way, we will be more than hurt; we may well feel devastated.

Sue and I were recently having a barbecue on a delightful summer's evening at the home of some friends. As I munched a hamburger off the grill from the brick-built barbecue just completed in the garden, I looked around. They had bought an old house and restored it beautifully. They had carved a garden out of the wilderness. Peter said, 'Well, this is what it's all about really, isn't it? We've got our home how we want it now, and I'm concentrating on building up sufficient security through the business. Some day soon I shall free myself from responsibilities and just enjoy it all.' I smiled a rather sad smile and gently said to Peter that I didn't actually think that *was* what it was all about. It was really quite hard to convey how profoundly I disagreed with the direction in which he had set his heart.

Oswald J. Smith was a man with a burning ambition to share the good news he had discovered. He viewed this project as the best investment he could make:

You are laying up treasure in heaven or upon earth. Everything you have you must ultimately lose. Everything you invest in the souls of men, you will save. You are going to enter heaven either a pauper, having sent nothing ahead, or as one who is to receive an inheritance, made possible by contributions laid up while still upon earth. (Oswald J. Smith, *The Challenge of Missions*)

Living in the light of heaven means holding even your most treasured possessions lightly. They may have great financial or sentimental value to you. But you know that the essence of your life is not really locked up in them. They can be enjoyed for what they are, but the moment we attach too much significance to them, we shall be in great danger. If our heart is anywhere other than in heaven, it is not where God designed it to be.

Material things are not the only area in which our heart may be misplaced. The higher things that this world can offer in culture, books and music can also capture our hearts to an exaggerated extent.

The books or the music in which we thought the

beauty was located will betray us if we trust to them; it was not in them but through them, and what came through them was longing. These things – the beauty, the memory of our own past – are good images of what we really desire, but if they are mistaken for the thing itself they turn into dumb idols, breaking the hearts of their worshippers. For they are not the thing itself; they are only the scent of a flower we have not found, the echo of a tune we have not heard, news from a country we have not visited. (C. S. Lewis, 'The Weight of Glory' sermon 1941)

After his clarion call to Western society concerning treasures in heaven, Jesus went straight on to tackle another subject which is still a problem in the twentieth century: worry. Living in the light of heaven, with our treasures stored there and our hearts in the right place, we have no need to get stressed about the necessities of life. 'I tell you, do not worry about your life, what you will eat or drink; or about your body, what you will wear' (Matt. 6:25). Birds don't go in for intensive farming or high technology storing of foodstuffs, but their heavenly Father feeds them. Do you not consider yourself more valuable than a common sparrow or a cawing crow, asks Jesus. Obvious answer: of course I am more valuable. Obvious conclusion: God will look after me too and I don't need to worry.

I heard a shattering thing a few days ago. A friend of ours had recently visited a missionary in Uganda. This faithful girl had left the security and comfort of England to live in a tough place in Africa, bringing medical help and relief to a desperately needy area as well as sharing the good news of Jesus with people whose spiritual need was just as acute. The devastating thing was that financial support for this missionary was so sparse that she had lived for six months on beans.

I don't know how many books are published every year or magazines every month whose sole concern is food and fashion, going into the minutest detail about how to please our palates or look our best in what we wear. A beautiful meal prepared with loving hands can speak volumes of devotion. We can probably all make the best of ourselves in what we wear, without being extravagant, and that is a pleasing thing. But I shall never forget that I could survive on beans. Frankly, I would rather do that if I felt there was any danger of the earth getting its clammy hands round my heart.

Sacrifices of an extraordinary nature have been made for earthly dreams. Nelson Mandela is one such hero of our time. He recalls in his autobiography, 'As a young man, when I joined the African National Congress, I saw the price my comrades paid for their beliefs, and it was high. For myself I have never regretted my commitment to the struggle, and I was always prepared to face the hardships that affected me personally' (*Long Walk to Freedom*, Little, Brown and Co., 1994). If this is only an earthly ambition, how much more should we be inspired towards our heavenly ambition?

I pray I will never forget my Boss's instructions and the guarantee that goes with them: 'Seek first his kingdom and his righteousness, and all these things will be given to you as well. Therefore do not worry about tomorrow' (Matt. 6:33, 34).

Since, then, you have been raised with Christ, set your hearts on things above, where Christ is seated at the right hand of God. Set your minds on things above, not on earthly things. For you died,

and your life is now hidden with Christ in God.'
(Col. 3:1–3)

Setting our hearts and minds in the right place diminishes
the appeal of unhelpful things. I sometimes wonder why I
am feeling less in touch with the Lord or spiritually dull. I
have often traced it to something read in a book, seen in a
movie, or dreamed in an idle daydream; thoughts which I
had allowed into my head when I should have locked the
door of my mind and put up a sign saying 'no entry'. At
a recent men's conference, the evangelist J. John urged us
all to put a little notice quoting Psalm 101:3 on top of our
television sets: 'I will set before my eyes no vile thing.'

The eye is the gateway to the heart. Every modern
advertiser knows that, but the Psalm writer knew it long
before they did. If you and I guard the gateway, following
Jesus will be so much easier. We will block the pathway
of many temptations before they even reach us.

Someone said that the darker side of the human
heart is like a keg of gunpowder, ready to explode
in destructive fashion if a flame comes near. Pouring
a bucket of water on the keg, however, changes the
situation completely. The same flame can ignite a few
dry bits of gunpowder it finds, but it will soon fizzle
out. Living in the light of heaven, setting our hearts
on things above, dampens the destructive possibilities
within us.

A heavenly perspective

Sometimes I get really fed up. Plans don't seem to be
working out, effort put in on some project seems to
be wasted, people I'm praying for don't seem to be
changing and, on top of all that, God has allowed me

a physical disability so that just the ordinary things of life can sometimes seem such an exhausting effort.

It is time to recharge the batteries and get everything in perspective. I take my little blue pocket New Testament from the corner of the shelf where it lives in my study and slip it into my jacket. Then I grab a walking stick and stomp out of our garden and up the hill behind our home. Ten minutes later I can be sitting on a log looking out over the tiny village where we live and before me spreads the panorama of the Weald of Kent. Way below the cars look like children's toys and people like ants. It feels as if you are on top of the world and looking down. I haven't really left my cares and troubles behind, but from this vantage point, life seems different.

I get out my pocket New Testament and turn to Revelation 7. It is time to do a little daydreaming of the right kind. If life has got out of perspective, the best cure is to get heaven into perspective. I read about John visualising millions of Christians of every nationality standing round God's throne in shining white robes. They all have smiles and they are having a great time celebrating. Waving palm branches, they are singing loudly, 'Salvation belongs to our God, who sits on the throne.' They have been delivered from everything bothersome and all the credit goes to God. I dream of joining them one day and think how good God is at rescue operations.

There are a few thousand angels standing around too. Face downwards before God's throne they worship, 'Amen!'

Praise and glory.

And wisdom and thanks and honour.

And power and strength . . .

be to our God for ever and ever.

Amen!

Seven items of praise making it all perfect and complete. I join them in spirit. Then one of the heavenly beings in charge, tells John some wonderful things about this massive crowd. They have come through terrible troubles and hard lives. They were sinners like the rest of us, but their clothes are shining white because Jesus has washed out the sinful stains from their tainted earthbound life-clothing and so they are dazzling white.

They serve God day and night.

God protects them in every way.

They have no more worries about earthly appetites or physical circumstances.

They are absorbed with enjoying the company of Jesus.

His springs of living water provide total satisfaction and fulfilment.

All these millions have finally arrived. Their deepest longings, achings and searchings have melted into untold joy.

I stand up from my log and dust down my clothes. Heaven is back in focus and the heavy weights of earth feel lighter. I take a final glance at the last phrase of the chapter: 'And God will wipe away every tear from their eyes.' The suffering, hurts and sorrows of the world seem to cry out for all this to come true soon. 'Are you coming soon, Lord?' I muse to myself. I take a peep at the last verses of Revelation before putting the New Testament back in my pocket.

'Yes, I am coming soon.'

'Amen. Come, Lord Jesus,' I whisper. I walk down from the hilltop with a lighter heart to resume the God-given privilege of living in the light of heaven.